Vantage POINTS

HOW TO CREATE A CULTURE WHERE EMPLOYEES THRIVE

PAULA LEACH

Published by
LID Publishing Limited
The Record Hall, Studio 304,
16-16a Baldwins Gardens,
London EC1N 7RJ, UK

info@lidpublishing.com
www.lidpublishing.com

A member of:

businesspublishersroundtable.com

Printed by Gutenberg Press, Malta
ISBN: 978-1-911671-00-8
ISBN: 978-1-911671-22-0 (ebook)

Cover and page design: Caroline Li

Vantage POINTS

HOW TO CREATE A CULTURE WHERE EMPLOYEES THRIVE

PAULA LEACH

MADRID | MEXICO CITY | LONDON
NEW YORK | BUENOS AIRES
BOGOTA | SHANGHAI | NEW DELHI

CONTENTS

With respect and appreciation for my Dad.

Coming from a council estate and leaving school without qualifications to being senior manager in a multinational company, you are my inspiration for everything I have been driven to achieve. You didn't need to read a book on leadership – throughout your career instinctively you were humble, kind, practical, celebrated others and were much loved for your sense of both integrity and fun.

ACKNOWLEDGEMENTS

Firstly, a huge thank you to the team at LID Publishing for helping me to bring a set of thoughts and ideas, which have been forming together for about three years, to life in this book. Thank you to Alec Egan and Martin Liu for believing in the project and to Aiyana Curtis, Susan Furber, Caroline Li and the editorial and design team for helping me to streamline and make the written work better. It's been a learning curve and I have much appreciation for all the help, guidance and belief.

Thank you to my friend Natasha Wallace who runs her brilliant coaching practice Conscious Works and is the author of *The Conscious Effect*, another great title published by LID. We discovered our shared ambitions for writing and our shared passions for compassionate leadership, and as I helped you build the momentum for your book, I have taken momentum from your brilliant journey to help me complete mine.

To Professor Vlakta Hlupic, thank you for your immediate connection and energy to the book and for your wonderful endorsement and encouragement! We know we share a deep purpose to help build human-centred, kind and joyful working cultures. Let's continue to be part of changing the working world together!

In 2017, I had the very great privilege of meeting the powerful duo of Baroness Margaret McDonagh and Lorna Fitzsimons, as I embarked on The Top Flight Leadership programme run by these wonderful, impactful and deeply kind women. Through the programme and the network of brilliant people I met, this opened up a world of new opportunities and adventures which I just didn't even think would be for someone like me. You helped me to dream big and to believe in myself. This book is just one of those adventures which I may not have even thought possible without that confidence boost.

To my gorgeous daughters Natascha and Sophie. Watching you grow into empathetic, ambitious young women is just pure joy. You have had to put up with your Mum disappearing to write or edit or juggle my multiple professional interests for a few months now. And I do realize that when I think I am talking to myself in my head as I compose the writing of a thought or the formation of an idea when cooking the dinner, I am really talking out loud. I realize you also think this is either funny or just weird. Remember that you will turn into me one day, so full of ideas they bubble out of you in conversation with yourself!

Finally to Martin, my partner in our life adventure. This book is written fundamentally because, over those long Friday evening discussions when we catch up over a glass of wine about our week, you listened to and discussed and supported the development of my thinking. For over 25 years you have believed in me and have encouraged me to find my voice way beyond any belief I have in myself. Your support is unwavering and you have always enabled me to have the space to be creative and take leaps of faith.

INTRODUCTION

WHAT'S *YOUR* VANTAGE POINT?

You might be the CEO of a global corporation, or you might be the founder of your own passion project. Perhaps you are in the middle of the management hierarchy of your organization, or maybe you are leading a small, tight-knit team of experts. Wherever you find yourself as you pick up this book, I am going to encourage you to make the most of your unique position and to leverage the opportunities you have to see things others can't for the good of the overall shared endeavour.

I've spent over 25 years embedded in the private multi-national, large-scale public sector and in rapid-growth entrepreneurial businesses. My passion and my purpose are helping everyone to fulfil their potential, play to their strengths and feel free to contribute their best to collective, meaningful work.

I've watched and worked with many leaders over the years. This has led me to think deeply about the point of leadership and why we aren't always optimizing human potential in organizations.

My conclusion is that every leader – no matter whether you have thousands of people working with you or just one – has two main responsibilities:

- To create direction and clarity – to ensure shared understanding of expectations
- To get out of the way – to enable and support the creativity and activity of others

In this book, I aim to help you consider your unique vantage points as a leader and provide some practical examples and tools for **CREATING CLARITY** in a simple way. Additionally, this book will help you to understand that **GETTING OUT OF THE WAY** is purposeful and productive, and requires skilled mastery in nurturing the potential in others.

WHAT IS LEADERSHIP?

LEADERSHIP IS ABOUT ENABLING AND SUPPORTING OTHERS TO GET FROM A TO B. All leadership is about outcomes, whether they involve making a product or providing a service. Even spiritual leadership is about an outcome – helping others to move their mindset and thinking from A to B. Leadership is about getting to B – or, rather, transitioning something from today's state (A) to the state of tomorrow (B).

LEADERSHIP IS A CHOICE. Leadership is not a position or something we can impose on others. Leaders are there to inspire and generate productivity, collaboration and creative agency in others.

Much has been written and researched about the humble leader, or leader as servant. We have models outlining different leadership styles and approaches. We can test ourselves, receive feedback and expand our range of responses. All this is very good and helpful, and, to put it as simply as I can, I think of leadership as a privilege, where others may choose to follow.

LEADERSHIP CAN BE SHARED. The job of any leader is to unlock the potential of others and harness this to achieve something, be it a move from A to B, an attempt to create and innovate, or a way to generate gains. All of this has nothing to do with the leader and everything to do with the others who choose to follow.

LEADERSHIP IS A PRACTICE. Carol Dweck talks about the difference between a fixed mindset and a growth mindset in her book *Mindset*.[1] Many people see leadership as a destination, a finishing point or point of arrival. And sadly, with a fixed mindset based on personal achievement, they stop being curious and enquiring, or challenging themselves and seeking feedback and help from others. In my experience, the strongest leaders are those who recognize that to seek and take on leadership responsibilities is to seek to accelerate growth, achieve flexibility and continuous learning, and source support and help. We could think of the idea of 'practice' as being constantly vigilant and purposeful in order to ensure that our actions and behaviours are serving a purpose.

CULTIVATING YOUR VANTAGE POINTS

"A vantage point is a place from which you can see a lot of things."[2]

As I have thought about leadership over the years, I have continually returned to the following image, which ultimately resulted in this book.

The visual looks something like this. Imagine a leader, coordinating a team of people picking crops in a field.

First we see the leader **IN AMONGST** the team: observing, asking questions, listening and connecting people together.

Next, imagine that leader stepping back **TO THE SIDE AND AROUND** the edge of the team, to the edge of the field, looking in towards the team, and looking adjacent to the field to neighbouring fields, woodland and grazing pasture.

Third, notice the leader climbing up a ladder to a high crag at the side of the field, walking to the edge and looking **FROM HIGH ABOVE** down to the field and observing the activity in the field.

Next, we see the leader, in that same position but looking **FROM HIGH OUT AND BEYOND** the field towards the horizon and the mountains in the distance, the local towns and the movement of people and vehicles along the pathways and roads.

Finally, the leader takes a deep breath, sits down and closes their eyes to enable them to look **INSIDE**. They notice their own feelings, instincts and emotions, and draw on their experiences.

Over time we observe the leader moving between all five of these vantage points. This image led me to consider that there are five vantage points that every leader must be conscious of to ensure that they are optimizing their unique position. The leader has unique access to these vantage points, and it is important to spend time in each on a regular basis to support the work of leadership.

The leader uses and moves between places that provide different information, perspectives and insights into the same situation – in this instance, a group of people picking crops in a field. In my mind, this image looks something like *Figure 1*.

FIGURE 1: THE VANTAGE POINTS

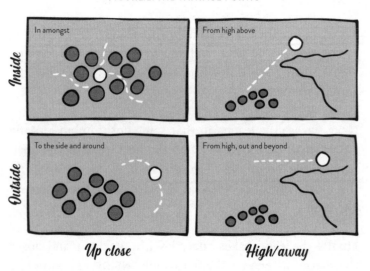

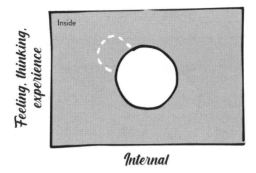

Internal

You might not work with teams of people picking crops in a field – I never have – but that doesn't matter. This is just a way of visualizing the idea that leadership is all about awareness. Given the meaning of the phrase 'vantage point' at the beginning of this section, this struck me as a simple and appropriate term to use to communicate my concept. I purposefully refer to vantage points (plural) because seeking awareness from multiple vantage points creates the ability to connect everything together and develop a systemic understanding.

By cultivating multiple vantage points, each leader can fulfil the two main responsibilities of leadership by creating clarity for their team and getting out of the way. *Figure 2* shows the job of the leader as these two key responsibilities, such that this clarity and support enable the team to move the outcome from A to B.

FIGURE 2: LEADERSHIP

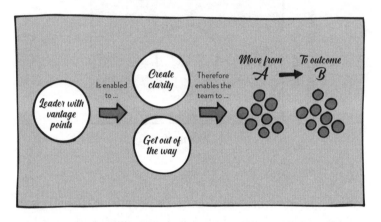

Part One of this book explores our five vantage points, looking at them in more detail by continuing the focus on the scenario laid out in this introduction. We will consider the definition and characteristics of each and how to move between them.

Part Two of the book looks at the pursuit of clarity. Clarity is obtained and enhanced by using all five vantage points. This section introduces some models and approaches that will help you as a leader to use your vantage points to create more clarity.

Part Three explores how, as a leader, you can practice getting out of the way. Getting out of the way is all about creating space for others to thrive and take action, and providing support to help them do so. We will explore how understanding yourself and other people allows you to build motivation, encourage collaboration and deliver results. Understanding the five vantage points is integral to cultivating a leadership practice where you are more able to create space for others.

Part Four pulls together a useful toolkit that can help leaders to bring these vantage points to life in the everyday. This is a list of 12 key tools or methods that leaders can try to see which ones they find helpful or useful when focusing on this way of leading teams. They are extremely practical and provide leaders with some tangible ways of working to bring these concepts to life.

WHAT HAPPENS WHEN LEADERS DO NOT CREATE CLARITY AND GET OUT OF THE WAY?

Lack of clarity and direction can lead to inefficiency, lack of shared endeavour and potential for conflict as different individuals and groups pursue varying agendas. For the most part, these agendas are undertaken with goodwill, but they can lead to frustration and a lack of productivity and progress.

Failing to get out of the way means the leader often fails to create the space for others to create, solve problems and take action. Empowered teams, with space to deliver and grow, are more likely to harness their collective potential, solve problems quicker, innovate faster and deliver to a higher standard.

Clarity and getting out of the way are mutually dependent. It is extremely hard to get out of the way without sufficient clarity. Without a clear shared direction and parameters within which to operate, the leader is needed for lower-level decision-making, resolving conflict and communicating between teams. Clarity enables a leader to get out of the way. Similarly, how can a leader create clarity without first getting out of the way? The leader requires the space and ability to see the bigger picture and take into account different points of information in order to create clarity. This is difficult to do unless they are somewhat removed from the day to day operations of the team. They must use all of the vantage points to see systemically and have the time and information to create high-level direction. Leaders must cultivate both simultaneously. *Figure 3* explains this mutually reinforcing opportunity that leaders have. The extension of this is that the more a leader does of one, the more they can do of the other.

FIGURE 3: CLARITY AND GETTING OUT OF THE WAY

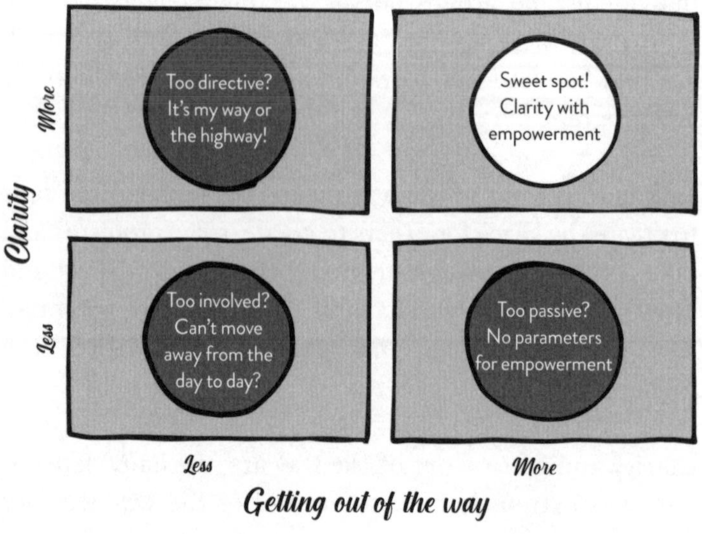

Getting out of the way

12

Another way to understand these two jobs of the leader is to think of the job of leader as that of a butterfly, with one wing representing clarity and the other representing space. Both need to be attended to and developed together in a leader's practice in order to achieve balance. With beautiful symmetry, the butterfly is able to flutter and fly, thus performing its role in the ecosystem and making everyone's lives a little brighter with their flight.

PART ONE

Exploring Vantage Points

Chapter 1

A LEADER'S FIVE VANTAGE POINTS

I have introduced the five vantage points that are available to any leader in any organization, regardless of the scope of the leader's responsibility. In this section, we'll explore each of the vantage points in more detail.

IN AMONGST

DEFINITION: the leader is seeing things up close and is right alongside the people participating in the tasks that represent the work that needs to be done. This vantage point is **SHARED** with others because what you can see as a leader, others can also see. The work that needs to be done means the tasks and activities that propel the team or organization forwards in pursuit of a strategic objective.

EXAMPLES OF ACCESSING THIS VANTAGE POINT:

- Walking the 'floor'
- Doing the work alongside – participating in the activity
- Workshops
- Looking at how work gets done (process flow, hand-offs between team members, duplication, quality standards, daily output, etc.)
- Health and safety walks
- Skip-level meetings (meeting with employees at least one level removed from your direct reporting line) or focus groups
- Mentoring

THREE THINGS THIS VANTAGE POINT GIVES YOU AS A LEADER:

1. Being in amongst is of critical importance to you as a leader because this is where you understand what is working, what is not, how people are interacting, whether tasks are being done efficiently, how people feel, whether there is sufficient clarity about what people are doing and why, etc.

2. There are opportunities to actively move between observation and coaching at the micro level to help explain clarity and direction within the context of the work that needs to be done and not just as a concept.

3. When a leader sets direction, it is of utmost importance to know whether the interpretation of this direction is (a) understood by those undertaking the work that needs to be done and (b) supported by individuals and the team because they see it as having meaning and being realistic

in the context of the work that needs to be done. The only way to know this is to be up close, in amongst and open to listening.

THREE RISKS TO BE AWARE OF WITH THIS VANTAGE POINT:

1. Sometimes there is a risk of spending too much time in amongst. This can be a particularly risky prospect for a leader if they have been promoted from inside the team. It could feel safer, more comfortable and familiar. Friendships could exist that draw the leader in. Too much time here risks the leader not getting out of the way sufficiently.

2. Similarly to the above, not only is it a risk for the leader to spend too much time in amongst, but it is also important for them to consider what they are doing whilst they are there. If the leader starts to perform the tasks of the group, or provide too much oversight and authorization, then the risk is that this is not a vantage point at all for the leader. Rather, they may get pulled into doing the group's tasks and activities as an additional layer of supervision. The leader may find themselves reinforcing and 'telling' people about their stated direction rather than observing whether this has been understood and supported, and reflecting on how best to build that feedback into the next version or course correction. The role of the leader in amongst is to coach and observe such that adaptations to clarity and direction can be made. The leader's intervention occurs through the provision of clarity and direction, and not through doing the tasks. There are two exceptions to this. Firstly, in an emergency where all hands are on deck, a leader might join in

with the work to support the team and be a resource or to provide very directive instructions for the short duration of the emergency. Secondly, a leader might actively practise observation through doing – for example, in a 'back to the floor' experience where they actually practise certain job roles in order to further their experience and understanding, with the idea that this should serve them in the creation of clarity and direction.

3. The final key risk with in amongst is the risk that it could become 'in amongst people like me.' The leader constantly needs to be vigilant to ensure that, when in amongst, there is variation and diversity between different teams, individuals and functions. This is critical in ensuring that the vantage point of in amongst does not contain blind spots.

TO THE SIDE AND AROUND

DEFINITION: the leader is seeing things up close to the work that needs to be done but is slightly removed to the side and is fully observant. In this vantage point, there is no specific interaction with those completing the tasks and activities. In addition, in this vantage point, the leader can not only see inside the team or organization but also into the surrounding environment on the ground – this may be an adjacent team, a competitor's activities and performance, etc. This vantage point is **NOT SHARED** with others because what you can see as a leader, others would need to be invited by you to see. Others may experience their own version of this vantage point by removing themselves from the activity and actively observing from the side. However, unless invited by you to observe the same activity and dynamics at the same time, they will see something different to you.

EXAMPLES OF ACCESSING THIS VANTAGE POINT INCLUDE:

- Doing your work whilst sitting in an open-plan office with your team
- Performance data and quality data
- Attending meetings as a listener (if you are a teacher or an educator, you will be extremely used to being observed in your teaching; if you are a call centre operator or a sales executive, you may have your calls monitored – this practice can be extended by leaders attending team meetings or other such forums not to contribute, but simply to listen)
- Employee surveys
- Recognition schemes
- Analyses of competitors and their performance
- Monitoring efficiency of communication and hand-offs between activities in the value chain of your organization (e.g. between production and sales)

THREE THINGS THIS VANTAGE POINT GIVES YOU AS A LEADER:

1. This is a uniquely special vantage point because you have access to your team and the environment where the work gets done (note that this can be a virtual environment – the key point is the access that you have as a leader). However, what is different to in amongst is that, by staying to the side and around, you are not influencing the responses and activity that you are experiencing

and seeing because you are not interacting with them. Imagine that you are.

2. You have the peace to reflect. This vantage point can be quite hard to prioritize and maintain as it may feel the most passive. Being close to the action but not interacting with the people or the tasks directly can seem like a lost opportunity to be in amongst. However, spending time actively listening, watching and observing in this way removes you as the leader from having to express yourself and enables reflection and focused observation. You will see and notice things that are fantastic and things that are interesting and that inform your role, providing clarity and direction that you would not gain from anywhere else.

3. You can invite others to reflect with you. Whilst this is not a shared vantage point, it is the easiest and most responsive in terms of inviting others to observe alongside you. This will help with your potential blind spots and will create a new sense of perspective and shared endeavour. Gather a small team and look at performance data or employee survey data together.

THREE RISKS TO BE AWARE OF WITH THIS VANTAGE POINT:

1. Take care not to stray from the side and around to in amongst. There is a big difference between these two vantage points, which are both 'up close.' It is entirely valid to move between both; however, this needs to be done consciously and it is difficult, particularly for extrovert leaders or leaders who have an active learning style, to remain in observation and not start to interact.

2. Ensure that you are looking both ways. The value of being to the side and around is that from this perimeter-based perspective, you can see inwardly to the team and the activities therein, whilst you can also see sideways, which may mean to other teams, other organizations and the surrounding environment on the ground. For example, in a retail environment this could mean watching the customer experience in the store next door, and in an internal organization it could mean noticing how a team interacts and communicates with the team working in the next stage of the organizational value chain. Looking both inside and outside will prompt opportunities for reflection and understanding, leading to decisions and action.

3. When does observation feel like Big Brother? The best practice here is that observation and listening need to feel and be experienced as positive and constructive. Therefore, they must be done with the knowledge and consent of the group, and the leader needs to over-communicate what they are doing and why. If the 'why' is to check up on performance and productivity, then expect a number of things to start happening, including people 'gaming' what you see so as to be seen as performing, and 'playing small and safe' so as not to risk any form of deviation from your direction. Listening into a group without their knowledge or permission may be considered spying and will erode hard-earned trust, fast. Conversely, try to practise listening to comprehend and understand whether direction and clarity require course correction or communications require stronger clarity, and reinforce this with strong behaviours – such an approach is invaluable to a culture of trust and engagement with leadership.

This is the potentially riskiest vantage point in terms of your relationships with your team because you are highly visible in your observations and if those observations lead to repercussions that feel negative for individuals or the team, you will lose the value of this vantage point in helping you to set clear direction and correct your course.

FROM HIGH ABOVE

DEFINITION: the leader is away from the specific tasks and activities of the work that needs to be done and is taking a vantage point that looks from high above to see the team's activity and dynamics holistically. This vantage point is **NOT SHARED** with others but it does of course offer the opportunity to invite others to see the organization from high above. But it is important for the leader to know that they will uniquely see things others will not see unless invited.

EXAMPLES OF ACCESSING THIS VANTAGE POINT:

- All data and information across the organization and team, from performance metrics to external metrics
- Access to meetings and decisions with key stakeholders outside the immediate team (peers, bosses and sometimes external influencers)
- Looking at how work is done (process flows, handoffs between team members, duplication, quality standards, daily output, etc.)
- End-to-end processes, efficiencies, and opportunities for greater synergy and collaboration

THREE THINGS THIS VANTAGE POINT GIVES YOU AS A LEADER:

1. The most important perspectives this vantage point offer the leader are the holistic view and the contextual view. The leader has the ability to see the activities and tasks of the team in relation to other influencing factors and opportunities. This perspective and access to this wider information enable the leader to create joined-up processes, ensure that communications are consistent and drive towards a common purpose.

2. From high above, the leader can look for inefficiencies and avoid duplication across teams. They can also ensure that the work that needs to be done is prioritized and delivered without unnecessary inefficiencies.

3. At this vantage point, the leader is able to help explain the 'why' by clearly seeing the connections and context of the work that needs to be done.

THREE RISKS TO BE AWARE OF WITH THIS VANTAGE POINT:

1. It can be lonely up there. One of the key risks of being high above is not keeping this vantage point exclusive to yourself as a leader. One of the great opportunities of leadership is to share what you can see and invite others to participate such that you can help to explain decisions or reasons why (e.g. explaining why collaboration with another team is essential). Sharing data, having a team member shadow you and inviting a team member to attend a key meeting alongside you are all ways of sharing this vantage point.

2. The leader doesn't realize that this is a vantage point. This may sound odd, but many leaders run the risk of spending their time in amongst and to the side and around whilst not realizing that one of the main differences between their position and that of their team members is access to this vantage point. So a leader may attend a corporate meeting or have access to data, but, if they do not see this as a unique opportunity to view and continually improve the operation and impact of their area of responsibility, then there is a risk that all that valuable insight will be lost from the whole team.

3. Insight and information may not be interpreted for use. Having access to information or a perspective that provides a systemic understanding must lead to interpretation of that insight in relation to the activities of the team and *the work that needs to be done.* If this higher-level, contextual understanding is not pragmatically leveraged by the leader (e.g. communicated, or built into decision-making, data analysis or business cases), then it is interesting but not of value to the activities of the organization. So the vantage point must result in an insight that is shared or actioned.

FROM HIGH OUT AND BEYOND

DEFINITION: as in the from high above vantage point, the leader is away from the specific tasks and activities of the work that needs to be done. In this instance, they are taking a vantage point that is SHARED with others in the sense that other leaders at this level and in other teams (or across other industries) can see from this perspective as well. Therefore, this prompts opportunities for networking and exploring the perspective with outsiders to the team. Instead of looking at the work of the team and the work that needs to be done, the leader raises their eyes to the horizon and seeks information that is external. Unlike to the side and around, where an external perspective can also be sought, this vantage point enables a much more strategic viewpoint. Whilst this is not a shared vantage point with others in the direct team, the leader can invite others to share and build an understanding of this perspective.

EXAMPLES OF ACCESSING THIS VANTAGE POINT:

- Wide reading in journals and executive media
- Networking events and industry or subject-matter briefings
- External data (competition analysis, national statistics, etc.)
- Conferences and webinars
- Memberships and affiliations
- External coaching and mentoring
- Legal and political awareness
- Awareness of financial markets
- Interest groups and social dynamics

THREE THINGS THIS VANTAGE POINT GIVES YOU AS A LEADER:

1. The primary opportunity with this vantage point is to build an external understanding that can help you navigate and anticipate changes, for example in demand or industry conditions. This enables the leader to keep ahead and ensure that this information is guiding and

shaping their organization's direction (and ultimately the work that needs to be done).

2. There is stimulation to be creative and innovative. Cross-industry information can be valuable, for example in helping to create shifts in a product's positioning or attracting an untapped customer base. This vantage point provides access to best practices from industry colleagues, other organizations and cross-sector comparators.

3. It provides the opportunity to grow. It is largely in this vantage point that the leader themselves grow and develop. Exposure to a wide variety of briefings, insights, networks and discussions will ensure the leader doesn't stand still in their own development and learning.

THREE RISKS TO BE AWARE OF WITH THIS VANTAGE POINT:

1. The leader might never get here. This is likely the main vantage point that will fall by the wayside when calendars are busy. This vantage point offers a longer-term benefit – the problem is that, all too often, we never get to that longer term because we are living in the short term. Leaders must prioritize this space for their perspective to grow.

2. The vantage point is not shared with others internally. Colleagues and team members are likely to be allowed to experience the stimulations relevant to this vantage point (e.g. attending conferences or having time for research), but there is a risk that the leader's (or others') insights from the vantage point will not be explored or shared in any meaningful way. So the insight is held within the person who experienced the perspective,

and not enough time or space is given to sharing and considering potential useful applications of the insights.

3. The leader stays safe with their tribe. There is a very large risk that the value of stimulation and building curiosity that can be gained from this vantage point will not be realized because we tend to continually attend the same conferences with the same people and read the same publications. The opportunity exists to challenge ourselves as leaders, really using this opportunity to say 'yes.' Whilst we should ensure we are accessing information and insights that we can readily digest and leverage from trusted sources, we should also broaden our perspective. For example, if you are an operations leader, attend a diversity conference, or if you are a marketing and sales leader, read the *Financial Times* or attend an event targeted at another industry sector.

INSIDE

DEFINITION: this is my favourite vantage point, partly because it is so simple and completely accessible all the time, and partly because we so often undervalue intuition when, in fact, it is one of our most valuable assets. In the inside vantage point, rather than observing outwardly to help guide decision-making, communications, direction setting, etc., the leader ensures that some space is available for internal reflection. We have all had those moments when we wanted to just take a moment to consider new information, or reflect on some dynamics in a team to help us with the right intervention (if any intervention!). Inside is also valuable in enabling the leader to be fully aware of their own self and, therefore, their impact in any given situation.

EXAMPLES OF ACCESSING THIS VANTAGE POINT:

- Going for a walk
- Meditation or breath work
- Journaling
- Coaching
- Sleeping on a decision – unconscious processing
- Using self-assessment tools to understand preferences, motivations and impact
- Active listening
- Gut instinct
- Experience

THREE THINGS THIS VANTAGE POINT GIVES YOU AS A LEADER:

1. Time. One of the most important opportunities with exploring inside is that there are no external demands upon you or distractions. It gives you the opportunity to mull over certain problems, opportunities or ideas. Creating time for this kind of reflection isn't difficult but it must be a conscious choice. If someone needs an answer from you, unless there is something critically urgent, there is usually time to thank them for the input and the question, and say that you would like the opportunity to reflect.

2. It is an opportunity to check in with yourself to ensure that you are acting in service of others. As outlined in the introduction to this book, leadership is about others.

We are, however, all emotional human beings with our own responses and preferences. Therefore, the opportunity to reflect inside enables us to pause and check in with ourselves to determine whether our responses and decisions are based on our needs or whether we are acting in service of others. Developing this practice is vital for compassionate leadership.

3. We all have experiences that are valid and that shape our instincts and intuition. We all need to check in with ourselves from time to time to process data and information gathered from other vantage points, to consider a decision, or to reflect on how to communicate something. When we do this, we can rely on the reference point of our own experience from past situations. Experience and gut instinct are incredibly strong and usually have good foundation for reflection.

THREE RISKS TO BE AWARE OF WITH THIS VANTAGE POINT:

1. We are one person with inevitable unconscious bias built into the fabric of ourselves due to our life experiences and how we view the world. Inside is extremely valuable, but taking it on its own without other vantage points can lead to us pursuing decisions or practices that run the risk of not being inclusive.

2. Inside is best when some of it is shared. Effective leaders are prepared to be open, vulnerable and able to share their thought processes and the space that they create for reflection. They are able to step others through the reflective process so it is not invisible and feels more transparent.

3. The leader may lack sufficient self-awareness or self-confidence to trust their intuition or instinct. Data rules in many workplaces and many people are conditioned to overemphasize data and objective argument. Whilst this is important and of course extremely valuable, so are experience and gut feeling, and in fact these are very much part of evidence-based practice. Leaders need to feel sufficiently confident in themselves to value spending time inside and creating the space to do so. They also need to cultivate self-awareness in order to build the skills required to notice and be able to differentiate between emotional and rational responses. Much of the work involved in getting out of the way is based on and rooted in self-awareness.

MOVING BETWEEN VANTAGE POINTS

The idea of the concept of vantage points is that this is a dynamic practice for leaders. The invitation is to consciously understand that there are five different and often unique places from which to view and consider the work that needs to be done and the team dynamic. You can then consciously choose to spend time moving between these vantage points gathering value and insight such that, as a leader, you can perform the two simple but critical roles of creating direction and clarity, and getting out of the way.

PART TWO

Creating Direction & Clarity

Essentially, any leader who seeks to create direction and clarity must describe (1) the parameters within which the team performs their activities and (2) the destination the team is headed towards. It's a little bit like painting a picture. Doing so creates shared ways of describing things because everyone is looking at the same thing. By using all five vantage points, the leader has the opportunity to create a sense of shared momentum. I have split the creation of direction and clarity into three stages:

1. **SCENE-SETTING**: drawing the outlines and boundaries that show where we are headed (Chapter 2)

2. **COLOURING IN**: providing more shape, colour and texture (specifics) in the scene (Chapter 3)

3. **SHARING THE VIEW**: communication and comprehension (Chapter 4)

For each of these stages in Chapters 2–4, I will outline ways in which each of the five vantage points can enable leaders to create clarity.

Chapter 2

SCENE-SETTING

What is scene-setting? Put simply, it is the leader's ability to describe, very succinctly, the direction of travel. It is like drawing the outline of a picture.

There are four main questions to answer when scene-setting. All of these benefit from including as many people as possible. Whilst it is the leader's job to create direction and clarity by setting the scene, engaging as much experience and as many different perspectives as possible will create a much richer, more informed and more inclusive picture. Not only does involving people make sense because there is greater pooled knowledge and experience, but it also means people are invested in the way forwards. Consequently, they will buy in to the successful adoption and implementation of any decisions and direction rather than having to have those decisions and directions communicated and 'sold' to them later on. It also avoids the need to be directive during the implementation stage as people do things because they want to rather than because they have to.

QUESTION 1: WHERE?

This is probably the most fundamental question for any leader to be able to express. It is the origin of all vision and mission statements, strategies and organizational design. Yet it is often far too complicated and therefore loses power, impact and energy. Sometimes the process to try to define it is never ending. The key here for leaders is to let go of trying to achieve the perfect description with all the answers, and to go simple and directional. The question is 'where are we going?'

If we recall our five vantage points as outlined in *Part One*, the leader primarily needs to be focusing on from high above and from high out and beyond to draw an outline of where the team is headed. In the spirit of inclusion, as mentioned, the leader may invite others from the team up to the higher vantage points to see those perspectives, help make sense of the environment and thereby help to make the decisions. Examples of this in reality might be sharing data or inviting others to a meeting involving a wider group of stakeholders.

What is required is not a fixed destination with every question answered – what is required is a sense of direction, with a visual description of what where we are going looks like.

The key point is that the leader needs to believe in their description of where they are going, which brings to the forefront the importance of the vantage point of inside. It is critical that the leader can share and talk about where we are going with belief and passion.

QUESTION 2: WHY?

Be driven by purpose. I can't add anything to the literature on the question of purpose and 'why' – Simon Sinek has that covered![3] It is vitally important for everyone to understand and be fully invested in why we heading in a certain direction. It becomes the North Star when we gets lost in the dark, and the roots when the branches of decision-making are swaying in the wind. The key point about purpose, however, is that it has to be felt by each individual. Connection to the purpose of an organization or any endeavour needs to be rooted in belief.

This is an area really worth spending time on and going deep. Asking 'why?' – and relating it to 'where are we going?' – will be the foundation for the shared endeavour of teams and groups that the leader is aiming to mobilize.

It might seem a very simple question – to ask 'why?' and to provide the answer. However, it is important to think about how a leader can leverage the five vantage points when asking this question. The leader's 'why' may not resonate with everyone – perhaps it requires too much explaining and needs simplification, or maybe there is a contrary 'why.'

QUESTION 3: WHAT?

Having determined where we are going and why, we must set that in the context of the present because this effectively creates the 'delta,' or the difference between where we are today and where we are heading. This means we can start to mobilize ourselves to take the steps required to move from A to B. The question fundamentally has to be answered with a description – a 'what.' The vantage points that are most required to understand and contextualize where we are today against our plan for tomorrow are in amongst and to the side and around. But the inevitable consequence of starting in these vantage points to determine the future direction is that there isn't systemic and wider data and information, so the opportunity to reach beyond current practice doesn't move far beyond continuous improvement. Consequently, many organizations find themselves rooted in incremental and slow change rather than bold, visionary ambitions. Not every organization needs to be fundamentally changing all the time, but setting the scene involves, as a first step, seeing the scenery from the higher-level vantage points and looking for the wider possibilities, free of the roots and current practices of today.

Bringing all of this together, leaders can use all four of these vantage points alongside the 'where are we going?' and 'why?' messaging to test their current practice. In doing so, they can do three things:

1. Take the opportunity to invite ideas and challenge and test the direction by seeking the opinions of those who will need to implement the steps to achieve it

2. Practically explain what 'where we are going?' actually looks like and what it means

3. Generate an understanding of the difference between where we are now and where we are going such that we can move our concentration from the start and end point

descriptions at either end of that process (where are we today and where do we want to be tomorrow), and start to focus our attention on the work in the middle.

By consciously using the vantage points of in amongst and to the side and around, leaders are able to take scene-setting to a very practical level of clarity that not only outlines a high-level statement of intention but also then moves the organization to reference and anchor this in the present so we can start to find a route to get there.

QUESTION 4: WORK?

At this point of scene-setting we are driving towards a clarification which brings meaning to the 'where,' 'why' and 'what' and turns this into a practical form. What is the work that needs to be done where we are going (and on our way there) and why are we doing it?

This moves the clarification on to a new level of granularity. The point of clarity is to enable everyone to understand and share in the direction such that they are all on the same page. Therefore, a distant vision of the direction is not enough – we need to bring it into sharper focus. This can only be done, however, after the previous three questions have been answered. Just as the description of where we are going must require us to look out and beyond the current practice, the last step in scene-setting, like the step before, benefits from leveraging the perspectives of in amongst and to the side and around. The intention of the question here is slightly different from Question 3. Here this is to take the high-level definitions of where we are going and the delta between that and where we are now, and to outline the work required to perform in these contexts. This should build a straightforward understanding of some of the skill shifts and priorities that are required during these stages of mobilization in order to achieve what we need. This information will be vital in setting the scene for the next level of clarity, which is all about 'colouring in' some of the detail.

Figure 4 outlines the process of moving through these four key questions when scene-setting, and the vantage points that are most useful and valuable for each question.

FIGURE 4: CREATING CLARITY AND SETTING THE SCENE
– THE FOUR STEPS

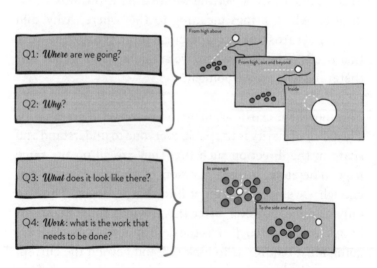

ONE THING YOU COULD DO WITH EACH VANTAGE POINT WHEN SCENE-SETTING

IN AMONGST. When scene-setting, this vantage point is helpful to build connection with the 'why' and the stories about it. Being with the individuals and teams and talking directly with them and listening will help to shape the language and the meaning behind the purpose of the organization and then also to test whether or not there is a shared 'why' that exists on an ongoing basis. It helps to reinforce some of the key messaging as to the 'why' and helps us to understand how this fits with other people's 'why.'

TO THE SIDE AND AROUND. From an observational point of view, you can be really curious – you can physically walk around and through workspaces and observe team meetings, and you can look at behaviours and artefacts (for example, the physical objects in a workplace which relate to culture – e.g. notices, artwork, awards). This can help you to understand whether or not the scene-setting is sufficiently embedded to provide shared direction and endeavour. It may be that there are meetings that have an agenda set up around a key priority (e.g. I recall a situation where an organization I worked for set the scene that health and safety was the number one priority, so every single company meeting started with an agenda item on health and safety). It could be that there are artefacts (such as recognition awards) aligned to a certain aspect of the scene (e.g. if innovation is part of your aim to create new efficiencies, a recognition award linked to this would be such evidence).

FROM HIGH ABOVE. With this vantage point you can see holistically whether the work that is being done is the work that needs to be done to fulfil the shift from A to B. You will be able to see – from macro data and patterns and reporting – where things are working and where they aren't. One of the best ways of achieving this is to have a set of business performance metrics that are designed to make it easy to understand whether the desired progress is being attained. For example, you can have a traffic light system (red, amber and green, or RAG) for various metrics so that you are alerted early to areas that are not on track for delivery within the scene-setting parameters (time, scope, quality, etc.). You can then to look to take action with the team, such as by reallocating resources, providing training, adjusting processes or realigning expectations such that they are realistic and achievable.

FROM HIGH OUT AND BEYOND. When scene-setting, arguably one of the most important vantage points is the leader's ability to see the work of the team or organization within the context of the wider organization, sector, locality or world. Referencing that external environment helps to shape the scene-setting. There are all sorts of models (e.g. external, competitor and market analyses) that leaders can leverage to assist in this process, but the essence is to spend time contextualizing the scene-setting for the work that needs to be done.

INSIDE. Sense-making and belief are the two key things to focus on when reflecting internally as you help to create clarity by setting the scene. It is important to keep in mind that a lot of information needs to be brought together to design an overarching picture. This requires reflection time to help you make sense of everything and to form connections. If you are a visual leader, you may find it helpful to draw how, for example, the move to a redesigned or new product will work alongside your company's existing products – visualize the portfolio. Belief is absolutely critical in this. If you as the leader do not have 100% commitment and belief regarding the scene you are setting, and you are not committed personally with your heart to the purpose or the 'why,' then you are going to have a difficult job leading the mission. Get clear with yourself by reflecting on how the 'where,' 'why' and 'what' make you feel.

Chapter 3

COLOURING IN

It is fantastic for you as a leader to have a clear direction to help you get from today to tomorrow and a vibrant and shared 'why.' But without the next level of planning, there is insufficient clarity within which teams and individuals can organize. Colouring in takes you from vision to proactive practical planning!

A leader's role is essentially to mobilize resources to achieve activities that move something from A to B. That can be running regular operations to create and deliver a product or service to a paying client or a beneficiary, or it can be moving the work of the organization such that the organization remains relevant, competitive and functioning during inevitable change. Usually, the job of the leader is both of these things in parallel.

Having set the scene, the outcome should be that there is greater clarity and shared understanding (and ownership) of the direction of travel. There should be a good understanding of what the work is that needs to be done – and why –

in order to ensure progress. How to (1) resource that work and (2) specify the work is the next job of the leader. If, when setting the scene, it was important to invite others to see from the vantage points in order to help with decision-making and direction-setting, then it is *paramount* at the colouring-in stage. The job of the leader at this point is much less directive and much more about coaching and enabling others to achieve clarity.

RESOURCING THE WORK

The information we have created so far in our scene-setting is the basis for our model – we can think of it a little like the foundations of a building or the structured undergarments of a fantastical period costume.

The first part of strategic workforce planning is to be able to express *simply* the information acquired during the scene-setting stage. This, essentially, is the 'what,' the 'where' and the 'why' of high-level work.

You need to be able to express this for today and for tomorrow. 'Tomorrow' could be one year or five years – depending on the planning horizon and what is relevant for you – but it should not be shorter than one year as this is a strategic clarification process. It is not regular resource planning, which is a more tactical matter – although it is enabled by a strategic approach being in place!

These are big questions, which ideally need to be expressed in three bullet points ideally. This will make the information clear and concise enough for regular repetition, yet easy for everyone to understand and to see the difference between today and tomorrow. As this strategic planning can be undertaken at all levels of an organization, the level of granularity will be relevant to the size and scope of the organizational unit.

STEP 1: WORK – TODAY, TOMORROW AND IN BETWEEN

Figure 5 outlines the first step relating to colouring in, which is the bridge between scene-setting and this stage of clarification. Essentially, we take the overarching clarifications with which we ended the scene-setting phase, which outlined the work at a high level. We now briefly explain, in very short bullet-point form (so it is easily repeatable and digestible,) the work today, tomorrow (e.g. one year or five years) and during the section in between.

FIGURE 5: CREATING CLARITY, COLOURING IN,
STRATEGIC RESOURCE PLANNING AND THE WORK

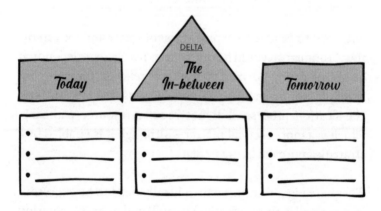

It is highly likely that the work that needs to be done today and tomorrow will seem similar, but there may be subtle or big differences in 'how.' Take, for example, a restaurant. Serving the customer their food would be the same today or tomorrow. But if our scene-setting had highlighted that we wanted to move to greater automation and self-service, then the 'how' of that work would look very different today than it would tomorrow (today, the waiter takes the customer's order and then coveys the food from the service counter to the table; tomorrow, an app takes the customer's order and a conveyor belt or automated robotic device delivers the food to the table). The in-between stage is also important. If we follow the same example, then during the transition from today to tomorrow, today's operational work needs to continue, but alongside there must be product design, testing, implementation and training. The job of the leader is to ensure that this is clear to the level of granularity required to ensure that shifts happen.

I have many times seen organizations doing good work when it comes to scene-setting. A strong strategic vision is helpful and can be shared widely. However, the next layer of granularity is either delegated by senior leadership to the next level in the organisation (and not described clearly enough). Alternatively, it may not be described at all because a perfect description of everything is required and this results in no action (because there is too much we don't know). Sometimes, we might need to choose one scenario to head towards (which could change) but course-correct along the way – this is perfectly acceptable and expected. Not moving at all because we don't have enough of the answers to be certain is not acceptable and does not fulfil our requirement to create clarity. Part of creating clarity is to acknowledge that not everything is set in stone, but, based on what we do know, the work will be as follows. This very clearly signals the general type of work required but also that it could be open to change as we move along.

STEP 2: RESOURCING ACROSS FIVE LENSES

Given that the leader is mobilizing a team to deliver a shared endeavour, the leader needs to concentrate on providing clarity for themselves and others to resource the work. So step 1 in the colouring-in stage was all about generating brief and quick descriptions of the work today, tomorrow and in between. Given that we now know what the work is that needs to be done, we can start the job of resourcing that work. Almost. The final requirement for creating the clarity at this stage is to ensure that the parameters for resourcing are understood and shared, and that the values and outcomes that the organization says are important are actually delivered through the micro actions within the organization. The way to create this clarity when strategic workforce planning is through the five lenses: financial affordability, diversity, geography, skills and wellbeing. I have distilled these five key lenses over many years of observing resource decisions and leaders creating clarity.

Many organizations and leaders will view resourcing decisions and direction as primarily financial tasks. Budgets are set, resources cost money and resourcing decisions are made based on the lens of affordability. However, as with most decisions, there is a sliding scale of affordability from the minimum viable to the maximum viable and, within this, we may weigh up other lenses and take account of the importance and value of each in the short and long term.

Leaders who believe affordability is a cornerstone of effective resourcing – but that it needs to be balanced with other aspects of getting the resourcing decisions right – will find they are much better able to deliver on the systemic range of important factors for their business.

The five key lenses need to be in consideration at the earliest stages of resource planning otherwise lasting and fundamental change will not be achieved. In the long run there will be a financial consequence to the organization, albeit in the short term paying attention to these lenses may feel like we are moving beyond cost minimization.

Data and being specific can help with clarity here. Often, leaders will make statements about the importance of diversity and the importance of skills, but fail to provide real, tangible parameters against which achievement can be measured.

Figure 6 sets out the five lenses that any leader who wants to create clarity for their organization should consider before putting in place resourcing decisions. Moving straight to resourcing the work that needs to be done without first establishing an understanding of the tangible and practical impact on the five lenses would mean we had no clarity as to the impact at all.

FIGURE 6: CREATING CLARITY AND COLOURING IN
– THE FIVE LENSES

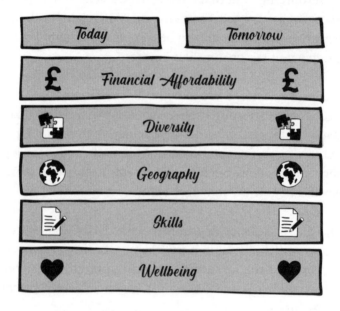

LENS 1: FINANCIAL AFFORDABILITY

Self-explanatory as this is, financial affordability is the main and often the only lens through which we have any clarity via specified goals or parameters. We have a budget for today and we often have a budget for tomorrow, and we might have a change budget for the in-between if there are incremental costs or parallel processes to track to achieve the change. In fact, in many organizations where the scene-setting has not effectively been clarified, the financial affordability becomes the scene-setting in and of itself. In order to ensure that the current state of budget allocation and availability of funding to resource the organization have been prioritized in the right areas, the leadership must take that first step back to ensure that financial resources are directed towards funding the work that needs to be done to support where the organisation is going, why and the what of the destination. Financials are clearly critical. There is no organization without the financials. But please, leaders, don't start here and don't end here.

LENS 2: DIVERSITY

Most organizations have moved beyond creating business cases to justify why diversity is important and why it is important to have a varied representation of people, whether in terms of is background or thinking style. This is now accepted as of critical business importance. Further explanation can be found in Matthew Syed's excellent book *Rebel Ideas*.[4] The challenge, though, is how to bring this idea to life. Many organizations will focus on initiatives, talent plans and recruitment initiatives; however, without clarity as to where we are today and where we want to be, we are searching in the dark and essentially we risk making resourcing decisions based on the other four lenses and inadvertently impacting our representation of diverse contributions without even knowing it or considering it. I am not a fan of targets from the perspective of making public statements about diversity ambitions – although they clearly have their place and in some instances do bring about action. (For example, the 30% Club in the UK was a campaign set up in 2010 with the aim of achieving a minimum of 30% female representation on FTSE 100 boards by 2015. By stating this aim publicly for accountability and working together to concentrate on taking action to make sustainable and meaningful change, the club achieved its objective by 2018.) However, I am very much a supporter of clearly stating desired outcomes in a measurable way. This informs and creates specificity around our ambition.

So, for example, we may want to ensure that we have more women in senior positions across our organization. To start, we need to know how many women we have in our organization today, at what levels and with what skills. We then need to ensure that we create an achievable ambition that is tangible and specific for tomorrow and demonstrates the shift that we say in our mission statements that we would like to achieve. Once we have outlined this, we can understand what the impact would be of certain decisions.

Let's take the example of a company that has three offices in three different locations. Office 1 has high representation of women at a senior level, Office 2 has very low representation of women at any level, and Office 3 doesn't have high representation of women at a senior level but does have good female talent coming through the organization – but we don't actually know any of this because we don't have the necessary data. For financial reasons we decide to close Office 3 and concentrate all our activity in Offices 1 and 2. Without data and specifics or clarity about where we are trying to get to (other than a broad statement about supporting diversity and female talent), we have just put back our achievement of our ambition, perhaps by years. The rising female talent was located in Office 3. Having the necessary data might not have changed our decision, but we could have put in place mitigation strategies to help support our ambition to move close Office 3 *and* keep a focus on female talent. By not having the necessary data as part of the debate and impact assessment at the time of decision-making, we immediately undervalued diversity versus our more specified and clarified financial objectives and aims. It could be in this example that, although Office 3 was at the stronger end of the financial impact range, we could have lived with the closure of Office 2 instead, still stayed within our financial tolerance and not harmed our diversity objective.

Having a strong and stated objective to achieve diversity helps to ensure that an organization's representation of varied communities does not inadvertently become impacted by other decision-making factors, costing the organization reputationally and financially in the future.

LENS 3: GEOGRAPHY

Second to financial affordability, specificity relating to geography and location is usually well serviced in decision-making and clarity in organizational resourcing. However, decisions based on geography and clarity about the intended future state demonstrate another good option for ensuring that there is clear direction on what this lens looks like in the future. As geographical and location decisions are usually not independent of other factors, this is usually a lens where other factors are the driver or are considered strongly. For example, geographical decisions are often made for reasons relating to financial affordability (e.g. off-shoring or locating call centres outside costly metropolitan city centres) or skills (e.g. locating next to a university town known for technical skills). Other key drivers for decisions relating to geography and location include the wider value chain of the organization and the need to support smooth inputs and outputs (with suppliers, customers, transport links, etc.).

But we can learn a lot about how we specify our future state with regards to geography and location by ensuring that we apply this interdependency to determine the right course for other lenses (and we can apply all five lenses to decisions related to geography). Many organizations re-evaluate whether their city centre locations are supporting the well-being of their employees or whether more dispersed hub locations or even full remote working could be supportive of wellbeing in the future. The risk with geographical specificity is that it can be a 'lag lens,' so we might have clarity about where we are going to be located in the future and why, but it is only there because of the financial imperative. Bringing the data forwards early and before resourcing decisions have been made may help us to ensure that we have taken into account all the impacts of a geographical decision and balanced this across the lenses.

LENS 4: SKILLS

Every leader knows that having the right mix of skills to resource their organization is absolutely core to delivery and their leadership responsibility. There is a lot of opportunity here to create greater specificity and clarity about exactly what skills are needed, and yet this is an opportunity many ignore. It is important to specify this for today, tomorrow and in between because building skills is usually a long game. Whether you as a leader are growing skills in your existing workforce or bringing in new skills, nothing happens overnight. It is vital to ensure that there is clarity and specificity about what is required, because work needs to happen all the time to generate the skills for the future proactively – skills simply cannot be delivered reactively.

The key to specificity with regard to skills lies in step 1 and why it is so important: what is the work that needs to be done? It is incredibly straightforwards to determine the nature of the skills required, the numbers of each different skill type needed and when the work needs to be done. When we aren't clear about the work that needs to be done, we can't be specific enough about skills and we will say things like, 'with the new systems we are introducing, our data entry roles will change and we will need people with higher-order processing skills to make decisions.'

What does that actually mean? It means we are introducing a new system and therefore job roles will change, but there is an intermediary and vital question: what is the work that therefore needs to be done? If we can answer this for today, tomorrow and in between, then we can build a skills plan.

This will help us to determine our actions for resourcing. Perhaps the people who perform an administrative function today do not need to leave the organization when a new IT system changes and takes over the work they have traditionally performed. We could reskill this talent given how much valuable knowledge they have about the wider organization and their networks. But how might they be reskilled? If we know the work that needs to be done in the future, we know what opportunities may exist so we can start early with the process of upgrading skills in order to meet the change timetable. Clarity on skills is vital and often missing at the appropriate level of granularity.

LENS 5: WELLBEING
You might be thinking that this lens seems a little 'soft' for a section all about clear, tangible data that demonstrates what we are aiming for such that we don't inadvertently miss it. Far from it! It is absolutely vital for leaders to understand how to build in specific measures that demonstrate ambition with regard to wellbeing so that is not excluded

from the design of their organization's resourcing. That is costly both financially and in terms of engagement. There are many sources of data that we can use to build up a picture of what our tomorrow ambition is for wellbeing: sickness absence data, mental health statistics, engagement survey data and attrition data, just to start. We need to pick three to five key measures of organizational wellbeing and then ensure that everyone in the organization understands that as we resource the team for the work that needs to be done, a thriving workforce is foundational to productivity. As a leader you must make sure that you always talk about the future-state organization not only in terms of its shape, size, make-up and location but also in terms of how it feels to be part of it as a team member. This will help you to ensure that you are very thoughtful about how to maintain and grow these factors as you build out your resourcing plan. Wellbeing is no less important than any of the somewhat more traditionally quantitative elements or lenses of our resourcing landscape.

SUMMARY OF THE LENSES

These are the five lenses every leader needs to understand. Being able to specify what 'good' or 'the future' looks like will allow us to collectively balance the priorities of each, weigh up the impacts of decisions by focusing on different lenses, and ensure that we take a balanced view of resourcing our organizations for the work that needs to be done.

Clarity for the leader is about setting the scene. This is then demonstrated throughout the organization by colouring in that intention and providing very straightforwards but balanced information and parameters within which the team can operate. This avoids losing sight of aspects that are important by becoming skewed towards one lens more than another.

STEP 3: SO WHAT DO WE DO WITH THIS CLARITY? THE LEVERS WE CAN PULL

What is the point of creating clarity for a leader? The point is that this clarity creates action and joined-up momentum, with everyone moving in the same direction and possibly faster due to their shared understanding. When resourcing for the work that needs to be done, this is a moment when a leader can bring together all five vantage points and ensure that any resourcing approach is both strategic and tactical at the same time.

There are only four levers available to any leader to pull, or create action with, when resourcing an organization and ensuring that any team or group contains the right mix of people (and other resources, such as IT or physical resources) to get the work done and move from A to B. These levers are:

1. Resourcing: bringing people into the organization or team, or bringing in new IT or physical assets

2. Evolving: building and reskilling the existing people, or changing the IT or physical assets

3. Leaving: exiting people, or divesting IT or physical assets

4. Retaining: creating focused plans to ensure that certain people with critical skills have an active retention plan that is tailored to their needs, or to ensure that certain

IT infrastructures or assets are supported and at optimum performance

Figure 7 outlines the four levers available to leaders and how they can influence the clear make up of the organization's shape and size. We'll look at each one in turn, but of course the magic of this model is that these four levers are not independent; rather, leaders can use them to deliver the outcomes stated through the five lenses. Throughout the following sections, I focus on people as an example resource, but a similar approach could be used to look at technology or asset resources. It is critical to understand the interdependencies between the levers and how pulling each lever affects the outcomes clarified using the five lenses.

FIGURE 7: CREATING CLARITY AND COLOURING IN
– THE FOUR ACTIVE LEVERS OF RESOURCING ORGANISATIONS

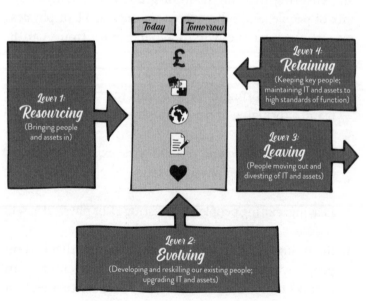

LEVER 1: RESOURCING

"The process of giving money, workers, skills, etc. to a particular job or piece of work."[5]

Bringing people into the team is a fantastic opportunity and is usually linked with optimism and growth. Organizations and teams recruit typically in one of two ways:

- **PERMANENT EMPLOYEES:** employees who are hired for a career in the organization and have the potential to develop and grow through multiple roles and functions in the business over time, adapting to the needs of the business and building their own capabilities such that they can contribute through deep mastery of expertise or through becoming leaders themselves.

- **CONTINGENT LABOUR:** individuals who are either self-employed or employed by or through a third party and provide labour that can be upsized or downsized quickly, thus giving flexibility to the organization or providing key skills that may be hard to obtain in the marketplace or may only be required temporarily.

There are variations on these two possibilities, and the opportunity I would like to present to you as a leader is to explore in full the widest possible breadth of the menu available for resourcing work in your team and organization. Some possibilities follow, although they are not exhaustive. Challenge yourself to look at your resourcing requirements from multiple vantage points and consider a fully blended menu.

Flexible, shorter-term resources:
- Temporary self-employed freelance labour
- Individuals sourced through a third party for key skills or capabilities
- Fixed-term hiring for projects or key short-term activities
- Interim roles (good for work associated with transformation)
- Full-service team or a managed service – i.e. hiring a full team through a third-party employer to undertake certain activities integrated into your team and business (not outsourced)
- Online virtual project resources

Long-term resources:
- Graduate recruitment programmes
- External experienced hires
- Returnships – i.e. programmes that offer retraining and placements for ex-employees with experience who have had career breaks (these are great for promoting diversity and reaching individuals who may not currently have the requisite skills; with some investment in retraining and reintroduction to the workplace, this is a fantastic population to resource with)
- Part-time or flexible resources working different hours (good for affordability and diversity, enabling your positions to be accessible to a wider range of individuals)
- Ex-military recruitment – i.e. obtaining transferable skills from ex-service personnel
- Outsourcing contracts for specified work (it is really important to get the hand-off between the outsourced service and the work of the body of the organization specified and monitored appropriately; however, this is excellent for operational business processes that can be measured through key performance indicators)

Talent pipeline resources:

- Partnership talent-pipeline models where individuals are employed by another organization, trained in key skills, and deployed to your projects and teams with the option to permanently hire them in the long run (a form of blending flexible resource plus extended recruitment)
- Apprenticeships, which build deep mastery and practical skills (although you must understand the need to build in extra supervisory resources for pastoral and skill-building mentoring)
- Traineeships (as above, with consideration for supervisory resources)
- Internships and work experience placements – for project work and some key delivery (as above, with consideration for supervisory resources)
- University or college sponsorship programmes, which can allow you to identify key talent early and partner with those institutions to develop the skills of individuals whilst offering work experience to build the individuals up to become 'business-ready' employees by the time they graduate

As mentioned, these are not fully exhaustive lists. However, the key to determining which options you choose to resource your team and organization is to diversify your approach. Aim for a blend of different ways of resourcing the work such that there is a mix of flexibility around shorter-term key work, longer-term resources hired for their ability to change over time, and talent-pipeline resources to ensure that you always have access to the skills and abilities that you need. You can then match these resource requirements to the five lenses (you have clarity with regard to the outcomes that you are seeking, so ensure that your resourcing blend achieves these out-comes and is not just done for the sake of headcounts). Specifically, your resourcing must be affordable, must promote and grow diversity, must provide the right skills for your future state and must be in the right location (or be capable of remote or virtual working), and your organ-ization must be able to support the anticipated needs of this mix of individuals from a wellbeing and well-work perspective so they are able to thrive. Hiring people with different expectations from what you as a leader can real-istically deliver may be the source of ongoing tension or challenges, which can impact productivity.

Resourcing the work and pulling this lever as a leader involve some of the most critical decisions that you will make, and they are very important to colouring in. It is costly to recruit the right person, but it is even more costly to recruit the wrong person. Being as clear as possible about what the work is – and resourcing that – is the start-ing point. Using a blended approach ensures that not only do you pay attention to the resourcing of the work but you also pay attention to the resource make-up of the team so that it can operate from a place of harmony and opti-mal diversity.

Whilst the decisions made with regard to resourcing and pulling this lever are the responsibility of the leader, I would argue that engaging others in the team through the multiple vantage points is really important. If you view the work that needs to be done through multiple perspectives, then you can articulate the best possible blend of resources to meet the need. If you were only to view the resourcing need from the perspective of in amongst, for example, you would miss some of the higher-level systemic considerations such as the overall skill base of the organization – the longer-range, longer-term view that indicates the requirements for talent-pipeline resources.

Many organizations and leaders are driven in their resourcing decisions by short-term immediate requirements for work and projects to get done (hiring for these) and short-term cost-rationalization processes (recruitment freezes and exit programmes). I would rather see a breed of leaders aware of the work that needs to be done and how this is evolving in their organizations by effectively and continuously setting the scene and then ensuring that they are colouring in by constantly monitoring and maintaining a focus on resourcing. This is not a one-off activity. Rather, the whole process of managing these four levers is like driving a car: you are constantly monitoring each lever and adjusting for the conditions. And unless it is absolutely critical, a team of any reasonable size should never turn off the talent-pipeline resources aspect of its blended resourcing approach. Turn off flexible resources and long-term resources by all means when affordability is low, but always keep the pipeline slightly warm. When you look from the vantage point of from high out and beyond, undoubtedly there will be a requirement to have those resources available. Typically these are extremely difficult resourcing programmes to crank up and down nimbly as they represent longer-term investments.

LEVER 2: EVOLVING

"To develop gradually, or to cause something or someone to develop gradually."[6]

The second lever available to a leader to ensure there is clarity about resources is all about growth and evolution. This lever makes it possible to adapt and adjust to the work that needs to be done. In the section on the resourcing lever, I described the middle category of resourcing options as 'long-term resourcing' rather than 'permanent hiring.' The reason for this is to challenge ourselves to consider what these people really need to do in our organizations.

Even in an organization where the operation remains consistent over many years and seemingly nothing much changes, everything is changing all the time. All organizations sit within a range of change. At one end, this might mean reasonably static business propositions that look similar on the surface but are probably impacted over time by changing customer profiles and needs, technology advancement and supplier profiles (for example). At the other end would be industries and organizations that are significantly impacted by disruption in their sector, which may come from new entrants changing the rules, new technology or any of a number of other things. Whether it is slow continuous development or rapid disruptive change, there is one thing that is certain and that is that things will change.

If you as a leader have created the appropriate focus with scene-setting, you can create scenarios showing these changes in whatever format you anticipate they may take for your organization. In this way, you can outline the scenarios' outcomes in relation to the five lenses.

Whilst the information that clarifies where you are going in relation to the five lenses is valuable for resourcing, it is also extremely valuable in understanding the evolution of the resources that you have today. Supporting your existing resources should always be the starting point. This is why the interdependency of the four levers is so crucial – no resourcing activity should be undertaken without due consideration of the evolution that can occur in your existing resources – permanent resource, or those on a long-term contract, should not be static. If the hiring process is clear and intentional at the start, these resources should have agility and change inbuilt. The individuals need to be adaptable and capable of movement in their skill profile. It is not necessarily possible to expect full flexibility in this group with regard to geography (for example), although this can be the case in some circumstances. And, certainly, an individual's diversity profile in many respects will remain the same throughout their working career with your organization (although in some aspects there can be change, for example becoming a parent or carer, gender reassignment, marriage or civil partnership, and ability and disability). By understanding the evolution of your long term workforce and having clarity with regard to the skills profiles your organization requires in the future, you will enable those employees and team members to make choices. You will also allow employees to be supported in their skill-building and reskilling over time such that they are best able to carry out the work that needs to be done or even anticipate it.

Relevant investment in growth and upskilling opportunities can only be achieved with clarity. This helps organizations to ensure that all of their change programmes are supported by an appropriate definition of their changing and evolving skills needs. Regularly profiling the current population against the stated outcomes for the future, as defined through the five lenses, enables continuous adaptation as to where to invest with the growth and evolution of this population. This means that resourcing decisions can be targeted and only activated when the existing pool of resources has been exhausted in terms of its ability to meet the needs of the evolving organization.

LEVER 3: LEAVING

"To go away from someone or something, for a short time or permanently."[7]

As a leader, there may be three ways in which you consider you have experienced 'leaving' in your teams and organizations:

1. Attrition: people leaving the organization or team voluntarily because they have another opportunity or for some other reason

2. Exit programmes such as redundancy programmes (compulsory or voluntary)

3. Dismissal for whatever reason

In terms of clarity and colouring in, as a leader, you hold more agency in relation to the 'leaving' lever than any of the others. This is linked to the interdependency of the levers. If you use fixed-term resources, it gives you leverage to manage those leaving your team or organization. The same is the case for all short-term resources, who essentially should be hired with clarity over the expectation of them leaving built in to the resourcing decision and communications from the start. Leveraging more partnership options at the resourcing stage enables more options with regard to the leaving lever. So, if you view the achievement of managing the resources of your organization and resourcing the work that needs to get done as a holistic picture, the levers can work in concert to provide options not only for increasing the amount of resources but decreasing it as well. If your short-term resourcing does not provide you with options for decreasing the amount of your resources easily when you need to (e.g. when affordability is an issue, skills requirements rapidly change or geographies adjust), then you need to consider whether they really are short-term resources or whether you are paying a partnership organization or a resourcing third party a lot of money for what are effectively long-term resources.

LEVER 4: RETAINING
"To keep or continue to have something."[8]

Have you ever experienced times when one of the really key people in your team (whether from a skills perspective, a leadership potential perspective or even a diversity perspective) quit? In some cases no one sees it coming, and by the time the leader knows about it, it's too late. The individual has found another job, probably with more pay, and there is little that the organization can do to retain that person's skills and capabilities. I think the least-used lever in the toolkit of the leader when monitoring and managing the resourcing of their teams and organizations is retention. Some leaders go to the lengths of creating a list of people who form a 'flight risk' or managing retention by offering long-term incentives or some other financial reward. There is nothing wrong with such schemes. However, I would like to encourage you as a leader to more proactively consider and use the retention lever as you colour in the clarity of resourcing your team and organization, giving this lever as much focus as the other three.

This is really only possible when there is a clear understanding of the work that needs to be done and the desired outcomes, as understood through the five lenses. When this is clear, it is not difficult to consider where key people or groups require a retention approach. It is also really helpful to have data surrounding attrition, and to enable and help leaders to understand any patterns that need attention. For example, if we have an ambition to ensure that we have a societally representative proportion of employees with disabilities at all levels in our organization but our data tells us that disabled colleagues are leaving at higher rates than non-disabled colleagues at the level just before mid-management, then our ability to grow talent of all abilities for more senior positions internally is reduced. We might want to look at our retention approach for disabled colleagues at this level. Here, we would want to be leveraging our vantage points – for example, the aforementioned data would be gained from high above. We might also choose to move in amongst to talk to those people and understand what is happening, so that we can tailor a retention approach that makes a difference. The reason that disabled colleagues are leaving may be nothing to do with financial reward and instead be related to flexibility, travel requirements or skills building. It may be these colleagues are much in demand, highly networked and resourceful and are being offered brilliant alternative opportunities.

Retention is personal and it requires us to get deep into motivations and personal feelings such that we are able to ensure that the key skills and key people in our organization do not leave as 'accidental attrition.' We may have the best resourcing approach and be focused on bringing in great new talent, but if we are losing those skilled people faster than we are hiring them, we have a retention challenge to work through.

SUMMARY OF THE LEVERS

With this model, leaders can use scene-setting to create the parameters or outline of clarity. This then supports a critical element of colouring in, which is ensuring that there are the right resources in place, continually evaluated, to deliver the work that needs to be done. The outcomes clearly defined through the five lenses should help to ensure that everyone is aware of the nature and make-up of the organizational resources required, and this data and information will enable leaders to perpetually adjust and manage the four levers available to help them continually change their resourcing to match the organization's needs. *Figure 8* brings all of this together, from the scene-setting questions of where and why, through the five lenses that define the work and the outcomes, and the four levers available to change the shape and size of resources.

FIGURE 8: CREATING CLARITY AND COLOURING IN – BRINGING IT ALL TOGETHER

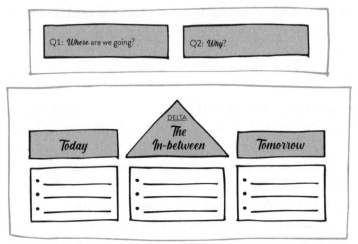

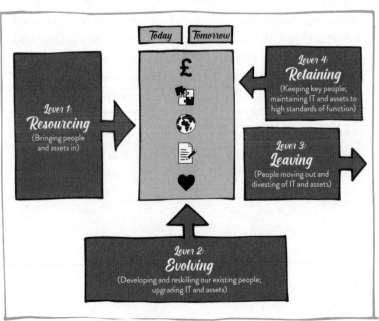

This model should also provide you as a leader with an understanding of the options available to you, the interdependency of the levers and the importance of using the vantage points when making your decisions.

Following are some examples of the kinds of scenarios that this model can help you to work on by providing clarity and helping you to colour in the picture of your organizational aims.

EXAMPLE SCENARIOS

TAKING A BLENDED APPROACH TO RESOURCING

With the clarity that comes with setting the scene and colouring in, I would encourage all leaders to think much more laterally than has often been the case in management and leadership over many years with regard to resourcing. We tend to think about resourcing our teams from one of two types of people: people employed by us (permanent labour) and people employed by others (contingent labour). Once you have better clarity over the work that needs to be done and once you as a leader are constantly evaluating the situation by leveraging your vantage points to understand the resources needed, you will open up a more varied and flexible pool of opportunities with regard to how to get that work done.

Thinking about the lists of possibilities outlined in the section above on the resourcing lever, there are lots of different opportunities to ensure that people are focused on the work. Why is this important? Often, organizations contain the same people, with the same jobs, year on year. Yet the work itself cannot be static. Therefore, think about resourcing as similar to the way in which tea is blended – making subtle and continuous changes and drawing from a variety of ways of bringing in the right people will make a difference. Workforce planning is the output of paying attention to the whole process of scene-setting and colouring in. Starting a workforce plan without this clarity fails to optimize the whole system and the team overall, because there is no continuous link back to the prioritization process and essentially to the 'where,' 'why' and 'what' – the purpose – of the team or organization. It is the leader's job to ensure that these vital steps are not missed out and that a well-blended resource plan is put in place *in response* to that clarity.

BUILDING TALENT FOR THE FUTURE

When I coach leaders, I am always interested in their approach to building talent in their teams and organizations. I often hear leaders talking about the fact that a core part of their role is to build and grow talent, and yet I would encourage more focus on these foundational elements by building clarity first. When leaders do not do this, there are three main risks that I see play out, none of which are desirable in the long run for the organization.

RISK 1. Without clarity with regard to scene-setting and colouring in, the leader builds talent based on innate and personal meaning attributed to talent, i.e. they build people like themselves. Focusing on building talent based upon an objective view of the work that needs to get done and therefore the skills required, reduces the risk of unconscious bias.

RISK 2. Without clarity with regard to scene-setting and colouring in, the leader relies on corporate standards and programmes alone as a proxy for building talent. These programmes are valuable – I have spent much of my career advocating for and building such programmes for future talent and leaders. They are often at their best when instead of focusing on ticking off requirements for future leadership positions, they are interesting for individuals as well as personally satisfying, because it is left up to each individual to determine the relevance to their own career and role. At worst, however, these programmes can feel irrelevant to the actual workplace. Sometimes this is because concepts are not exemplified using real-world expectations. In other cases, as I have seen a multitude of times, an individual has a brilliant experience at a leadership or talent programme, only to return to the workplace to a boss uninterested in their development journey and ill-equipped to reinforce learning through ongoing coaching. This can lead to the frustration of "I've seen how it should be – but that isn't how it is," and often only a small percentage of the learning is sustained over time. That isn't a great investment (these programmes can be expensive), and it delegates the task of developing the team and individuals somewhere else rather than the leader owning and marshalling the approach such that the resulting learning and growth are embedded and reinforced in the workplace.

RISK 3. Without clarity with regard to scene-setting and colouring in ... nothing happens. The intent is there, but without clarity there is no foundation or roadmap for talent so great words are spoken but people are not intentionally upskilled and developed for the work that needs to be done.

SUCCESSION AND TALENT PLANNING: A FIVE-STEP APPROACH
Succession and talent planning are primarily guidance – they are not set in stone but are methods of providing risk assurance to stakeholders, and they are a way of objectively

looking at and building talent in an organization. The clarity this brings for the leader and the individuals in the organization is very helpful. One of the main reasons people leave organizations is because they can't see a way through to progression and development. Succession and talent planning is hugely important in the toolbox of active retention and it is rooted in old-fashioned job analysis. I say 'old-fashioned' because in the past this area of practice has been associated with time-and-motion studies and control of work. My approach is that a very simplified version of job analysis really helps to create clarity and direction with regard to building talent. As a leader, you may have been involved in succession planning before. The point with regard to clarity and the models I have presented in this chapter so far is that this process often starts and ends with the completion of a corporate process rather than the leader really owning and driving the talent and succession plan. As we run through the five steps here in the process, please ensure that you leverage the clarity, and don't just complete step three.

STEP 1. Each organization has various job disciplines (marketing, sales, research and development, etc.). And within each job discipline, depending on the work that needs to be done, there are various job roles at different levels. Even in the most nuanced and creative organizations, where resources don't necessarily follow hierarchical organization chart structures, such job roles exist, albeit loosely defined and held lightly.

STEP 2. This can be done for the whole organization, but I would start with the most significant roles that either (a) are critical leadership positions that influence culture and are accountable for delivery or (b) are critical creative or highly skilled positions where those skills are absolutely key. High-light, using three to five bullet points for each position, the knowledge, skills, experience and behaviours that are critical for that job discipline or that role. It may help you to think about the incumbent in the position if there is one, but don't be limited by the way the current person executes the role from day to day. Rather, root the question in relation to the scene-setting and colouring in that you have completed.

STEP 3. Match the resources in your business (and potentially from your wider blended approach to resourcing) against the expectations outlined in step 2, classifying them according to whether they are emergency cover for that job role, ready now for the position, will be ready in three to five years or will be ready in more than five years. The result should look like a funnel, where you have more resources available for the role in your five-plus-years category. When it comes to emergency cover, one is enough. I find that using a traffic-light system (red, amber and green, or RAG) is very helpful here, particularly with large teams, to highlight whether you have a good, strong pipeline of talent in your organization to fill these positions.

STEP 4. Consider how diverse your talent pipeline is. Again, I advocate using a RAG rating as in step 3, but you could use a similar category approach or diversity representation, if that is your preference. You may simply like to look through the diversity lens to consider the range of skills, backgrounds and capabilities that are represented along your talent pipe-line. If you are not doing this with clarity at this stage of the colouring-in process, then you will not make a difference to your diversity representation over time intentionally. This is because you need this information, and everything else in steps 1–4, in order to achieve your all-important ambition, as expressed via data or specific targets.

STEP 5. Take action on the information that you have created through your succession and talent mapping. This action should be twofold and you can leverage the full range of vantage points to support you as the leader here. Firstly, take action individually. Every single person who features in a succession plan requires an intentional and two-way agreed plan for developing their skills, capabilities and behaviours. It is one thing to list people on a talent plan. However, without really focused guidance and clear next steps that are inspiring to the individual and that create shifts and changes in their capabilities and progression opportunities, then you (the leader) and the individual will retain the three risks outlined in the previous section. Secondly, take action holistically. Where you have red or amber highlights showing that your pipeline may not be as full, as robust or as diverse as you would prefer, then do something about it! This may be through returning to your overall scene-setting and colouring-in information, where you can see things through the five lenses and determine which of your four levers to pull harder.

Clearly, this is a large topic with opportunities for leaders to leverage their vantage points and really make a difference to the long-term, sustainable talent of individuals. This enables both individuals and organizations to benefit from clarity and action. *Figure 9* outlines this step-by-step leadership tool at a glance. If there is clarity with regard to expectations, the job of the leader is to facilitate the overall talent plan and then get out of the way by moving into a 'coaching and enabling' mode so that others can fill the space.

FIGURE 9: SUCCESSION AND TALENT PLANNING
– AN EXAMPLE TEMPLATE

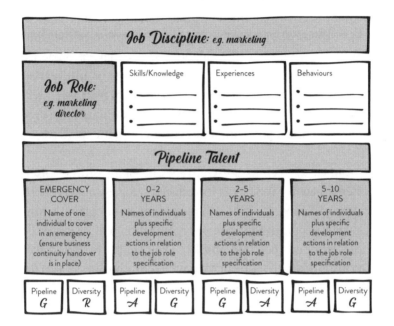

OWNING ATTRITION

One of the key aspects of this chapter's proposed model for resourcing the organization is knowing your data. It isn't about data for data's sake, but about using data in the context of all five lenses and all four levers to understand, where possible, what is happening. This is particularly helpful when it comes to attrition because there is often a view that attrition is something that happens to a leader that they need to react to, rather than something they can approach with much more intention. It is true that there will always be some aspects of attrition that are inevitably unintended by the leader and where a response or reaction is required (e.g. someone quits and you need to fill that role unexpectedly, or sudden changes to the market require you to enact a redundancy programme to make your resources affordable). My proposition for leaders is that the clarity obtained by understanding what is happening in this space (as outlined in the description of the third lever – 'leaving') is really valuable. If you have a proactive understanding, you can pull the other levers in anticipation to avoid situations where you are forced to act reactively. I will share two examples to illustrate this point, although there are many potential opportunities to put this idea into practice.

EXAMPLE 1. Technology changes and skills shifts. Often when a new technology is introduced – for example, robotization of a process – this will mean that skills currently provided by people in the team or organization will no longer be necessary and therefore obsolete. The simple linear answer to this is often the information which fills business cases for investment in technology: we will introduce the technology and save X number of jobs therefore Y amount of money.

All too often, however, these financial benefits are not realized in reality and I would urge leaders to use the clarity developed through scene-setting and colouring in to create a more positive and wider systemic picture of the impacts of change. Don't go linear. Go back to the work that needs to be done. Stay in the future state and, as far as possible, explain the work that will need to be done in the world when the technology is embedded. Chances are that whilst some processing jobs may no longer be required, other roles may be required to bridge the gap between humans and technology, interpret information or data, or carry out uniquely human tasks (e.g. quality control or customer service). Be realistic about the actual work that needs to be done in the future state, compare it with the today and describe the 'delta' – that is to say, the difference between today and tomorrow. This delta is like magic dust to a leader; it will enable you to do all sorts of things, such as provide much greater clarity with regard to the actual skills people will need and the specifics of how they could be retrained. It will also enable you to explain the future state to all stakeholders, including those in the team, and create a two-way dialogue about their future. This dialogue will enable individuals to feel part of key decisions and to look at options for themselves (such as upskilling, movement within the organization, or looking for new and different challenges).

That isn't to say that it will never be appropriate to introduce some form of programme to bring your resource levels in line with affordability. However, this clarity will enable you as a leader to think carefully about all four levers in the context of this decision and to own and manage attrition as a potential positive for individuals and the organization, not a negative. As shown in *Figure 5* (on page 46), the in-between stage between today and tomorrow outlines the opportunity a delta provides a leader to create even deeper clarity for decision-making and communication.

EXAMPLE 2. This example is linked to the section previously discussed 'building talent for the future'. Pretty much everything with regard to a leader's resourcing model is interdependent! (Think here of the vantage points of from high above and from high out and beyond, which enable leaders to see things holistically.)

Consider key top talent either being poached by others with better opportunities or having so little clarity on their path of development within their current organization that they actively use their own agency to seek out opportunities to develop at the pace and level that suit them. Fundamentally owning attrition in this sense is linked to leveraging a clear succession and talent approach where expectations are really clear, individuals can see the pathways and opportunities in the organization, and they are supported actively and openly to build on their strengths and develop areas that will enable them to use those opportunities.

There is no doubt that you will experience attrition from individuals seeking something fresh. However, creating an open and adult two-way dialogue based on clear understanding of expectations either (a) enables the leader and individual to feel committed to each other and to develop a plan for development that actually happens and that meets the individual's needs or (b) enables the individual to make a clear choice. In this latter scenario, the two-way, trusting conversation ensures the leader is alerted early to the individual's intentions if they do not wish to pursue the plan within the organization. The two parties can then mutually work on timings and plans such that the leader is rarely in shock and rarely has to go into full reactive mode.

THIS MODEL HELPS ANY LEADER TO GET OUT OF THE WAY

Given that the premise of much of this book is the importance of the symbiotic relationship between creating clarity and getting out of the way, this three-step model is a great example of how the creation of clarity can enable teams to perform and take action independently of their leader's constant intervention and direction. By stepping back, setting the scene and colouring in to this extent, and by leveraging the vantage points along the way, leaders can bring the team along on the journey of clarification by working through the steps together and 'sharing the view,' which we will come on to shortly.

There are so many other ways in which these methods of scene-setting and colouring in enable the work of leaders, including coaching for performance and active retention strategies. These few examples of how the model can create that all-important clarity for teams and organizations should help to illustrate the importance of making room for continual refreshment and for doing the work.

SPECIFYING THE WORK

We have talked about resourcing the organization and many of the ways in which a clarification approach can work by bringing together key data and a holistic view of the interdependencies of the various lenses and levers that each leader has available.

Alongside resourcing the work, the other key role of leaders in clarification at this stage is specifying the work. Whilst this is a large topic in and of itself with huge resources available to leaders to help them study and grow capability in this arena, I am just going to touch on two key areas of focus where leaders can ensure that their organization has the direction required to operate. *Figure 10* provides a brief outline which explains these two key areas that every leader needs to focus on once 'the work' has been defined. The two areas we will spend some time looking at to simplify this from a clarification perspective are programme management and setting expectations.

FIGURE 10: THE WORK

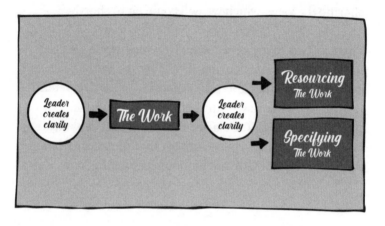

PROGRAMME MANAGEMENT

There is very little work that cannot be viewed through the lens of project or programme management. Even day-to-day operational tasks are essentially mini projects – anything that generates progress from A to B is a project. The job of the leader is to create the momentum within the organization or team to engage the people to create that progress from A to B.

Every leader in any position in an organization needs to have some level of understanding of project and programme management. I don't mean that everyone in leadership requires PRINCE2 or some other qualification and needs to manage all their work through a form of programme management software – these deeper methodologies and tools are helpful for those in critical roles in the organization who are involved in supporting leaders to manage the detailed plans, resources, progress milestones and problem-solving associated with the work. However, it is critical to have a high level of curiosity about the current methodologies that have been evidenced to make a difference to efficient ways of working for teams and individuals in support of the work that needs to be done.

Leaders need to understand their role in enabling others to work efficiently. This is because the way in which teams are set up in today's world of work – from the physical (or virtual) space that they need to occupy to the training that they need and the way modern agile resourcing teams are created – is often quite different from the way the teams may have traditionally been created to perform work together. This also has an impact on how structures work in organizations in terms of the need for more fluidity and flexibility with regard to working arrangements and reporting lines.

In the previous section, we discussed the opportunity presented to leaders to think in a more 'blended' way about resourcing their teams and organizations, and this is essentially the principle behind project teams. They lend themselves to flexibility and diversity, and taking a programmatic approach lends itself to creating clarity about the work that needs to be done. Projects always start with a very clear focus on establishing scope, and this discipline is nicely related to the point about ensuring that there is clarity about that scope.

There are two potential risks associated with building programme management into the regular discipline of leadership.

RISK 1. Too little exposure to the methodologies and actual training of programme management means that leaders might start to pick up on some of the language and approach but not understand them fully. The benefit of programme management as a tool in the toolbox for getting work done is that it very much plays to the point of this book, which is that multiple vantage points create a holistic picture. It is this idea that is the most benefit to leaders, so it is hugely beneficial to gain a deep understanding of the methodologies of programme management if you have not been exposed to them much in your previous experiences and roles.

RISK 2. Leaders can also have too much exposure to the methodologies of programme management. This is the opposite of the point above. Leaders deeply steeped in programme management experience and methodologies may be somewhat blinkered in their ability to see around the edges of the programme and understand the wider expectations of their role as a broader leader.

So, the point here is be educated, understand the value in the tools and the language, learn how to leverage programme management as part of creating clarity, but realize project management is not the only tool in the toolbox for leaders.

SETTING CLEAR EXPECTATIONS

I prefer to talk about setting expectations rather than setting objectives. Although similar, 'expectations' seems to me to be a broader term and also has the potential to be more inclusive from the perspective that two people can have expectations of each other. Setting objectives seems more one way as an activity. An expectation can be defined as "the feeling or belief that something will or should happen."[9]

Once the clarity has been created at a more holistic level by setting the scene and colouring in, then setting the expectations for individuals and groups is really key to enabling a leader to get out of the way. If you recall the diagram in *Figure 2,* which demonstrated the interrelationship between creating clarity and getting out of the way, setting expectations is right at the coalface of this work.

It is vital that expectations are rooted in the scene-setting and colouring in. From this perspective there is a strong foundation of clarity that should be shared by the leader and the individual or team. *Figure 11* outlines the importance of these foundations and then shows the two-way nature of expectation-setting with individuals and teams.

FIGURE 11: SETTING EXPECTATIONS
– FROM FOUNDATIONS TO EXPECTATIONS

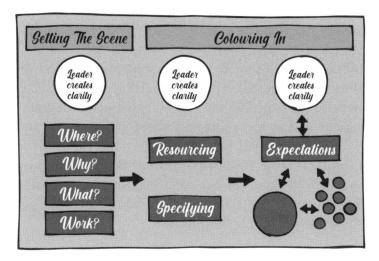

As with other aspects discussed in this book so far, setting objectives and ensuring there is clarity about what needs to be done is a well-researched area of management with many publications on the topic. In my experience, the methodology that organizations most commonly aim to put in place is SMART, where objectives should be specific, measurable, aligned/achievable, realistic and timebound. Keeping these key areas front of mind when setting expectations is really helpful, although the SMART approach only creates clarity with regard to the content of the objective. Leaders and teams need to ensure that there is a shared agreement that takes the SMART principles and goes a little deeper into real two-way communication about expectations. Two people may walk away from a discussion about SMART objectives having read the same words but having different interpretations of what those words really mean in terms of delivery. SMART supports clarity, but true overall clarity that is felt and owned by all parties is arrived at through both parties stating their understanding and sharing what they interpret and mean by the objective, thus sharing their expectations. Here are five key takeaways for effectively setting expectations.

TAKEAWAY 1. Ensure the foundations are in place. As already highlighted, expectation-setting for individuals and teams really does need to be based upon the foundations of the scene-setting ('where,' 'why,' 'what' and 'work'). It is only with these foundations that there will be a sufficient sense of shared endeavour or shared purpose on which to based further specificity. In addition, these foundations create clarity, which enables leaders to get out of the way during this process.

TAKEAWAY 2. Two-way communication is really important because the relationship between leader and team thrives when everyone feels heard. There are moments, particularly during a crisis situation, when one-way directive communication, with regard to expectations, is appropriate, and this will be readily accepted by all involved. But these situations are rare and, for the most part, human beings reach a consensus and solid shared expectations through conversation. The key to a good two-way conversation is ensuring both parties have the same information ahead of a meeting so they can discuss the matter and agree outcomes, and the leader should leverage all vantage points during that session to bring wider perspectives to the discussion where appropriate and also hold themselves in a place of listening. You may be familiar with the term 'compassionate leader,' which is "someone who shows kindness, caring and a willingness to help others."[10] Essentially, because the two roles of a leader (creating clarity and getting out of the way) are symbiotic and interdependent, setting expectations with a compassionate approach is essential and this can be achieved even in some of the most challenging discussions with a team or a team member through choosing appropriate language, creating empathy, listening and explaining your 'why' (purpose). *Figure 12* demonstrates the importance of compassion in setting expectations. The objective is to ensure that the team or individual and the leader are on the same page, moving in the same direction, and are absolutely motivated and empowered and feeling inspired to move forwards. The objective is not only to create clarity, but also to lift others up to move and progress. What I call 'clumsy clarity' is where clarity may be achieved, but the individual's needs are not attended to sufficiently such that, rather than being lifted up, they need to be picked up.

FIGURE 12: COMPASSIONATE LEADERSHIP
– AVOIDING CLUMSY CLARITY

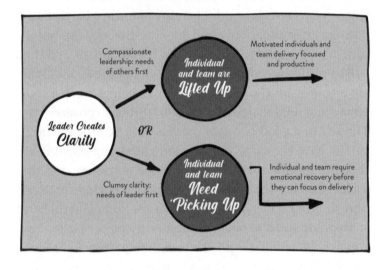

That is an example of a leader creating and communicating clarity for themselves, in order to tick the box to say that they have done so (e.g. "I told you what needed to be done" or "I've explained that to X person"). The point of this takeaway is that clarity is optimally effective in a leader's role of enabling individuals or a team to make progress from A to B when the individual or team are built up with compassion. The creation of clarity is for and about others. On too many occasions have I wondered why leaders don't pay more attention to this – we would reduce employee relations issues, create more harmony in team-working and have much less work for leaders on the whole if more priority were given to how people feel throughout and after a discussion on clarity as well as to the content and tasks at hand. We need to be compassionate and we need to lift up.

TAKEAWAY 3. In order to enable leaders to actually get out of the way, expectations need to be set by both parties such that the individual or team feel full ownership of that set of outcomes and deliverables. If there is not ownership, the intrinsic motivation to achieve the outcomes will not sit with the team, and the leader will find themselves continually drawn back into clarification. A couple of practical ways of introducing ownership to a team conversation might be:

- Together the leader and the individual or team look at the foundational elements of clarity (scene-setting and colouring in). The leader asks the individual or team to put forwards their version of deliverables that would further colour in what they need to do and how they need to do it to ensure progress is made with that foundation in mind.

- If the leader and the individual or team have slightly differing expectations or views as to the deliverables and outcomes, the leader needs to take a step back to foundational clarity and ask a question. For example, take a leader of a sales team discussing sales targets with an individual. The leader proposes a sales target, but the individual doesn't think this is possible. Firstly, space needs to be created for a discussion to take place. The last thing the sales leader needs here is an individual agreeing to a target that is unrealistic without saying so, as this will have a knock-on effect on many other aspects of the leader's remit and their own credibility. Secondly, the leader needs to understand why the individual doesn't feel that is possible. Thirdly, the leader has the opportunity to get out of the way and not step in with an answer to the individual's problem or challenge to the target. Instead, they can step back to the foundational scene-setting and ask the individual what they would suggest, if that target isn't possible but given that there is a need to achieve it for the business. This creates space for the individual to own the outcome in relation to the bigger-picture deliverables and expectations as per the foundational shared endeavour.

Both of these examples enable leaders to take a coaching perspective with regard to expectations, rather than directive. In this way, they can create the space for individuals to feel ownership of their objectives (this works with teams too).

TAKEAWAY 4. Start by providing the licence to colour in. As a development of the first example in takeaway 3, the leader can start by sharing perspectives with the individual or team by brining information and data associated with the various vantage points that the leader can access. The leader can then invite the individual or team to start by thinking about their ambitions for outcomes based on the parameters set with those foundational aspects of clarity.

TAKEAWAY 5. The great thing about diverse teams is that we all approach things in different ways. We solve problems from different angles, we work with different rhythms, and we are creative or delivery focused in different situations according to our motivations. Every leader wants to create expectations whilst holding on to as much of this individuality and difference as possible. Therefore, the key takeaway here is for the leader and the individual and team to agree upon the 'what,' but not upon the 'how' – so, there should be a focus on the deliverables and outcomes, but with the freedom to achieve those in the way that works best for the individual.

All these takeaways hinge on a couple of important aspects of setting expectations. Firstly, it is of the utmost importance that this whole process and approach is seen within the context of the entire system. Individuals may like to work a certain way or deliver through a certain method, but this has to be interconnected with the needs of others and the mechanisms others are using. So, for example, an individual who likes to work independently may prefer to achieve their outcomes by working remotely and just getting through their deliverables, but other team members may need to collaborate, understand what is happening and build upon this work, so the individual needs to manage their own expectations against those of others. This is true across any organization so it is important that resources are efficiently used and the whole system is taken into account. One of the key roles of leaders is to highlight through their vantage points these interconnected elements of expectation-setting and to build compromise for optimum capability and delivery.

The second aspect is that these takeaways enable leaders to use one of the most important tools in the toolbox of getting out of the way which is sharing their expectations not only about the work that needs to be performed and outcomes reached, but what the leader needs to know and when. A great example of this is often articulated by leaders when they talk to their teams and say, "Please let me know what is happening – I don't want any surprises." It is really important for leaders to create the right climate for a discussion like this to take place so that individuals and teams understand what their needs are. In this instance, explain why you have this expectation (for information and status updates for example) and it is likely to yield the right behaviours. A leader simply asking for status reports with no clear 'why' is not sufficient for the team or individuals to feel intrinsically motivated to help because they can't see the leader's vantage points (e.g. that meeting that you go to once per quarter where you need to provide a summary update on the team's delivery). When they know that is part of what you need to perform your role and support your stakeholders, the team will deliver this at an agreed frequency in an agreed format and you, the leader, can get out of the way in the knowledge that the individual and team will deliver to you exactly what you need.

SETTING EXPECTATIONS EXERCISE

I was fortunate enough to work with an experienced coach as I was building a team at one point in my career, and he shared with me the most simple – but most powerful – exercise for building expectations. This can be put in place between either an individual and a leader, or a team and a leader.

Figure 13 outlines this exercise but essentially the leader and the individual (or team) list (a) what they need from each other and (b) what they can offer each other. They then share their lists and create (or have a discussion facilitated to draw out) explanations of the key points, delve deeper into their understanding and create a shared sense of how to support each other with the work that needs to be done. Setting this alongside some clear deliverables based on the work that needs to be done creates a rich and shared agreement as to the 'what' and the 'how' of delivery.

FIGURE 13: SHARING EXPECTATIONS

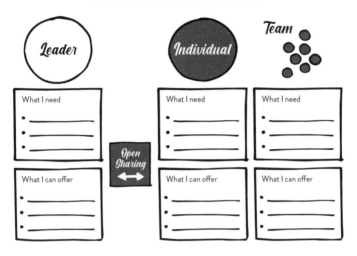

Why is setting expectations so important for clarity? This is the final stage in the toolkit that leaders can use to ensure that everyone has the same understanding, that there is an appreciation of everyone's perspectives and that the work can be done with as little interruption as possible. Clarity also enables performance and is the fundamental opportunity for a leader to create the conditions for high-performing teams and individuals. Without clarity, often individuals and teams can move in slightly different directions and move way from each other's expectations, which is costly not only in terms of time and money but also from a relationship and trust perspective. Leaders who invest up front in creating shared clarity and expectations in this way will have far fewer performance issues to deal with because alignment is reached before any interpretations are formed about the work that needs to be done. The final point about expectations and clarity as a whole is that this is an ongoing cycle of return and repetition of these methodologies to ensure that the focus is always bright and clear.

ONE THING YOU COULD DO WITH EACH VANTAGE POINT WHEN COLOURING IN

IN AMONGST. Test whether expectations are realistic and achievable by joining in. Get alongside teams, perform some of the tasks, get talking and listening, and find out with curiosity whether the theory of putting into practice this direction and these objectives actually works. Perhaps you will learn that the team could go further, faster. Perhaps you will learn that there are some skills gaps that have not been factored in and that need to be attended to and supported.

TO THE SIDE AND AROUND. Observation can enable you to understand whether the specificity in expectations that you and your teams and individuals have set is evident and working in practice. This will enable you to consider whether you need to enhance the specificity or change it, or if everything is running as expected.

FROM HIGH ABOVE. Get to know and understand your data as it relates to the resourcing of your organization. This is relevant in this vantage point because a leader's power to create clarity and be joined up about the impact of decisions and direction lies in them understanding where the organization is and where it wants to be in a measurable sense. This means understanding the data as it relates to the five lenses. (For example, what does the desired state mean in terms of diversity representation – do you want to match the official statistics on population representation for those who are economically active? In terms of skills, do you want a certain percentage of the workforce to be upskilled in a certain new technology? And what about creating a measurable for wellbeing – do you want a score of a certain percentage for employee engagement?) If you know your data today and you understand a range or estimate of where you desire to be, you can assess which of the four levers to pull and, within these levers, which specific blend of actions you can take that will best get you there.

FROM HIGH OUT AND BEYOND. Seek creative ways of building resources and evolving talent from external and broader sources. Start by being clear on the five lenses. Then if, for example, you are keen to build a stronger talent pipeline of people with disabilities to be part of your organization to meet your aims around inclusivity, you can look to other industries, best practices, professional support services and charities (for example) for help and advice to generate better and more creative solutions and options. You could use a similar approach if your colouring in had identified a skills gap in your resourcing model for the future. Looking from high out and beyond enables you to consider wider possibilities – can you find a talent partner to help you source those skills, or could you partner with a university or college and set up a sponsorship or apprenticeship programme to grow your own skills? Leveraging this vantage point when colouring in enables you to build in more creative and innovative possibilities.

INSIDE. Reflection is important in the colouring-in phase because this is the place where leaders most risk losing leadership focus, becoming task oriented and slipping into doing rather than being. Spend time reflecting on whether you are involving others sufficiently to share decision-making and direction and facilitating the filling of the space that scene-setting allows, or whether you are hogging the colouring pens. Reflect and check that you are guiding others to colour.

Chapter 4

SHARING THE VIEW: COMMUNICATION AND COMPREHENSION

One of the most critical roles for any leader is communication. People will be looking towards leadership for direction and clarity, but it is only once that direction is articulated in a straightforwards way that others can act upon it and generate movement, agency and shared momentum. Therefore, it is imperative not only that leaders articulate and share the direction, but also that this communication circle is completed and the messaging and information are understood. Comprehension is essential.

If leaders have been following the journey to clarity as outlined in Chapters 2 and 3, they should have built engagement with some if not all team members as clarity of direction was decided upon. I certainly advocate being open to sharing vantage points, building in the time and opportunity to learn from others, and ensuring that ideas and direction are tested. This chapter is built on the assumption that those things will be done. If engagement with team members has not been a feature of your scene-setting and colouring-in activities to this point, then time needs to be built in to the communication stage to fully explain the 'where are we going' and 'why,' in particular, and to allow time for people to give feedback and feel heard. Otherwise, you may experience undue resistance or just apathy or passivity – "We didn't help to shape this so we don't feel ownership of what happens next."

STAKEHOLDER MAPPING

You should ensure that a thorough stakeholder map is created to consider all individuals and teams, as they may require different forms of communication of the direction. The leader does not have to do all the communicating, but being clear who is communicating what to which stakeholders (and when) is really important.

Clearly, the identities of your stakeholders depend on what type of leadership position you hold. If you are in a significant leadership position in a large corporation, the stakeholders with an interest in your direction of travel will include external parties such as investors or analysts as well as suppliers and customers in addition to your direct team. If you are a leader within and organization responsible for the delivery of a particular team's contribution to a whole, your stakeholders will include other teams across the value chain of the business (for example).

All of us, whatever level of the leadership hierarchy we are at and whatever function or discipline we have a specialism in, are operating within a wider system. I have already touched on this with regard to setting expectations, and I will discuss it further in *Part Three* when I talk about seeing things systemically as a mechanism for getting out of the way as a leader.

From a clarity perspective, the importance of the wider system is relevant to appropriate communications. Being alive to and aware of the different stakeholder needs for information and insight into your scene-setting and colouring in, is important. Your job as a leader is to be ahead of the curve with regard to these needs and to be proactively thinking about all stakeholder requirements (and participating actively as a constructive stakeholder in other people's leadership endeavours).

Figure 14 provides a high-level example of a stakeholder map (note that it can be a useful exercise to literally map stakeholders with your team to help you share your vantage points). Such a map can help you to create clarity of expectation as part of the expectation-setting exercise towards the end of the previous chapter. Helping everyone to share in the anticipation of stakeholder requirements and needs is another way for leaders to create clarity and get out of the way.

FIGURE 14: STAKEHOLDER MAPPING

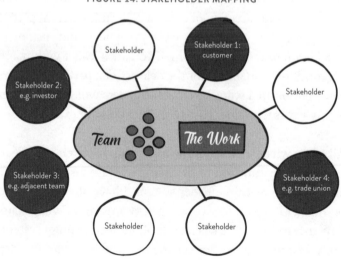

Mapping stakeholders is important in order to understand how the work of the leader and team fits into the bigger picture. The three key ingredients for effective stakeholder communications are:

INGREDIENT 1: CLARITY OF CONTENT. Doing the work of setting the scene and colouring in enables leaders (either directly or through their teams) to have clear content to share with stakeholders consistently and to gather feedback to evolve and adjust as necessary.

INGREDIENT 2: HAVING A SHARING APPROACH. This means two-way stakeholder communications where information is shared, but also feedback and insight are used as tools to develop further evolving clarity within the team. This also involves leaders and team members widely sharing the views and insights from stakeholders with each other so this information permeates the whole of the team.

INGREDIENT 3: ANTICIPATION OF STAKEHOLDER NEEDS AND BEING PROACTIVE. Thinking ahead of stakeholders' requirements and needs is really useful in building trust and effective working relationships. Stakeholder communication should be seen as an essential component of an effective team because a team is only effective if it operates successfully when joined up with the larger system.

All of these ingredients are brought together with the binding agent, which is clarity. If you know where you are going, why, what you are doing and the work that needs to be done, and this is set in the context of what is then actually happening and going to happen to make progress, then as a leader you have created the conditions for each of these ingredients to be activated and work well. Without that foundational clarity, there is no content to support these ingredients or principles.

WHAT IS BEING COMMUNICATED?

Different stakeholders will require different content to be communicated, so part of the stakeholder mapping exercise is to answer the question of what is being communicated (and, in addition, to enable feedback to gather needs and requirements from stakeholders).

Essentially, you should draw on the content generated from your scene-setting and colouring in. The two key perspectives to highlight when considering what to communicate to stakeholders are:

1. Relevance: what are the stakeholder's needs, not the needs of the originator? If there are areas where messaging needs to be sent out, this needs to be relevant and interesting to the stakeholder, so the content always needs to be woven into the particular interests and motivations of that stakeholder and their relationship with the leader and the team.

2. Simplification: the messaging needs to be focused around a core message that is not too complicated and is relatable.

HOW TO COMMUNICATE?

As with many other aspects of leadership, there are various ways in which leaders can hone their communication styles and I recommend developing communication as a regular practice. Seek feedback, watch yourself, practise delivering key messaging to ensure that you are succinct and learn how to tell stories that resonate. All of these practices can be studied and developed as part of the leadership toolkit of skills. Many leaders arrive in their positions expected to be able to present and communicate to a wide range of stakeholders and yet reportedly one of the most challenging experiences anyone can have in their life is public speaking. Many of us find it difficult and challenging, so we either avoid it or suffer much anticipatory stress. Asking for help and building up this skill are extremely important so that as a leader you have a range of effective communication mechanisms available to you through both formal and informal channels (and leveraging all vantage points to give and receive messaging so you can understand the place of your organization and team in the wider system).

REPEAT THE CORE MESSAGE

One tool is to develop a core narrative that is simple and can be repeated. Sometimes this can be in a visual format, or it can take the form of an acronym or a short phrase. This is similar to the concept of a mission statement. For the purposes of clarity, as a leader of any size of team, it can be useful to create a kind of guiding North Star – the 'where' and 'why' of your scene-setting, distilled into an easy-to-repeat and repeat-often phrase or mantra.

If effective, this will be adopted and repeated throughout your organization and will be extremely helpful for establishing the parameters that explain what the organization or team is and what it is not. Effectively, this is branding for a team, and it can have multiple uses across a stakeholder group.

INSPIRE ACTION, ENGAGEMENT AND COLLABORATION

Communicating as a leader should be all about inspiring some form of action, engagement or collaboration from others (stakeholders), depending on who they are. The action might be with regard to decision-making, or stakeholders might hold resources that would enable the team to move forward. It could be that the content that you are sharing is all about reaching out to engender a form of mutuality and reciprocity with information-sharing and collaboration from another individual or group. Communicating may be about creating the opportunity to build trust and a shared sense of direction that everyone can gather around, building a sense of community and purpose. Whichever of these are relevant (perhaps all of them), the key to note for leaders is that communication, as leadership, is not about the leader's needs. Communication is the means to something and it is the vehicle or route towards that end (whether it be inspiring action, engagement or collaboration). The answer, then, as to how to communicate becomes less about the needs and preferences of the leader and more about the needs and preferences of the intended audience or stakeholder, such that the messaging is experienced and heard as intended.

ALLOW TIME FOR SENSE-MAKING

Given, then, that it is necessary to communicate to be heard and with the audience in mind, a leader's communication approach and style must allow for sense-making on the part of the listener or receiver. Leaders need to ensure that they pay attention to the following themes and be attuned to all vantage points.

Firstly, leaders must build time for sense-making into their practice and their diary to enable the space and time for digestion of information, questions and clarifications as well as potentially multiple channels of communication for different parties and different stages of the sense-making journey. An example of this might be as follows. Say that a key stakeholder is a senior leader who has the decision-making authority to free up resources that are critical for some project work. The leader might take this communication in stages:

1. Content: ensure that there is clarity not only about the ask but also about the wider system so that implications and impacts on other parts of the system are outlined

2. Preparation: prepare a simple, high-level summary of the ask highlighting the request and the implications (this could be verbal or a short-written communication)

3. Detail: the simple summary should usually be supported by some form of documentation (e.g. a simple paper with an executive summary and further detail provided to outline the proposal)

4. Summary: include a short outline noting where agree-
   ments have been made and providing an acknowledgement or appreciation of the key stakeholder

Secondly, leaders must be ready to hear what others are saying and to adjust not only their communication method but
also the content based on what the recipients share back.
Note that they may not be consciously or intentionally
sharing anything with you. Say, for example, you are interested in collaborating with a stakeholder because they have
some data that would be useful to you. This stakeholder
may provide direct feedback about whether this is or is not
possible and maybe some feedback about access privileges
or other things that could influence whether the collaboration might be possible. Alternatively, the stakeholder may
simply not reply. Your request and communication may not
have relevance to them, so it is important to be prepared to
notice this possibility and adjust your messaging with the
needs of the stakeholder in mind.

Finally, leaders must be open to testing the effectiveness of
their messaging. Information overload is very often an issue.
Even if the stakeholder who is the intended recipient is in
the direct team of the leader, often communications are sent
via emails and people do not always read or fully digest the
contents because there is a lot of other 'noise' competing for
their attention. Leaders need to test whether or not their
intended messaging is actually being received and heard as
intended (and then consequently resulting in the desired
action, engagement or collaboration). Vantage points are
absolutely critical here, in particular in amongst for internal
stakeholders (as per the example), but all vantage points can
be relevant, depending on the stakeholder group.

ONE THING YOU COULD DO WITH EACH VANTAGE POINT WHEN SHARING THE VIEW

IN AMONGST. One of the most useful ways of working with this vantage point is to share the view by explaining. Share the view via communications and testing for comprehension directly with individuals and teams. Then, if necessary, add more communication and more opportunities for comprehension. Talk to people, understanding how they see their work and how it relates to the bigger picture. Reinforce some of the key messaging as to the 'why' and seek to understand how this fits with other people's 'why.'

TO THE SIDE AND AROUND. This vantage point offers leaders one of the best opportunities to do the real work of communicating, which is to listen. It can be hard, as outlined in the discussion of vantage points in *Part One*, to stay to the side and around and not jump in amongst. Jumping in is natural because we are social beings and we like the connection that in amongst provides. However, what to the side and around enables us to do is listen in two ways. Firstly, we can listen by observing with our eyes, ears and wider senses so as to create a better understanding of where we may need to adjust our work on clarity. Secondly, we can share that view with others, whether that is our direct reports, a team leader, a reverse mentor or any group of colleagues who are working in the team. Help them to stop being in amongst for a while and to see what you can see. Then listen. Ask questions and listen to the things that they observe, notice and share. That insight from sharing this view will be invaluable because rarely will they see themselves from this vantage point, but they also probably are the best people to create the adjustments to clarity that are required. Not only that, if they share the view, make observations and adjust the direction themselves, they own it. Your job was to provide the vantage point to others (which is a brilliant example of getting out of the way!).

FROM HIGH ABOVE. Building upon sharing the view to the side and around, I strongly recommend using exactly the same approach from high above. Sharing information with your team and organization about the team and organization as a whole helps to build awareness and connection with the scene and the bigger picture. For example, it might be clear that your team needs to improve its customer satisfaction rating because the data is telling you that it is not as high as you would aspire for it to be. In this case it is important to share that data (where the team is today), share where you want to get to, and invite the team to look holistically at the team or organization to collectively design the work that needs to be done to bridge the gap (to move from A to B). If you share the view (in this case share the problem) and invite others to raise their awareness, then this can have an impact on buy-in and also the understanding of the 'why.' I have seen it work well when organizations regularly brief the whole organization on business performance and the broader metrics. When this holistic view is shared from high above, people are better able to look at their own work and how it can contribute to the cause. This could include town hall meetings, regular communications, or team members shadowing you at a board or management meeting to observe and hear that level of discussion.

FROM HIGH OUT AND BEYOND. This section has discussed stakeholder communication and connection, and this vantage point is an opportunity to reach out to stakeholders and, again, share that view with others. This could mean attending conferences and events and bringing members of your team along to learn as well (and listening to what they are observing, noticing and taking in). It also involves leveraging the vantage point to clarify and stretch people's thinking about the scene-setting and how it is positioned. When you need to share the scene with stakeholders, you must build a pretty good script and story.

INSIDE. The reflection point here is all about simplicity. How simple and straightforward can you make the messaging? Is it so simple that you can repeat it over and over again? By personalizing the reason why you are telling a story and sharing a view, the story will be more compelling for your listeners and/or team. Leaders who can tell stories related to the 'why' build a sense of belonging and connection. Such leaders are more likely to continue to focus on communication and are motivated to share. There is also an excellent link here with getting out of the way and potentially sharing some vulnerability, which will build connection and engagement with others, who will then more readily buy in to the why.

CREATING CLARITY AND DIRECTION TOGETHER – SO YOU CAN GET OUT OF THE WAY

Although I have outlined the creation of clarity and direction via a three-step approach, in reality it is much less linear than this. Understanding that there are these three component parts is a bit like understanding three different dance steps and learning them individually. Once the steps have been understood and mastered, we know that the actual fluid dance movement is not a succession of learned steps done one after another, but rather an amalgamation of these steps in a blended expression in response to music. The job of a leader is to know these three steps, to understand and master them, and to learn to perform this work in a cycle and sometimes with a more fluid structure. *Figure 15* helps to visualize this. The actual work of the leader in creating clarity and direction is multidirectional throughout the three stages, with reference back to each of the five vantage points in a continuous process.

FIGURE 15: CREATING CLARITY
– MASTERING THE DANCE

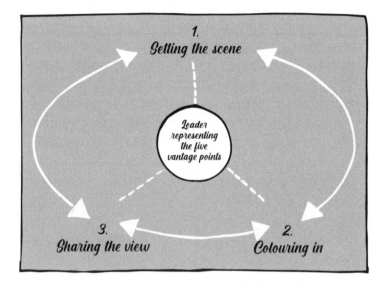

And because creating clarity and getting out of the way are mutually reinforcing, this leads us on to getting out of the way.

PART THREE

Getting
out of
The Way

GETTING OUT OF THE WAY
– WHAT DOES IT MEAN?

Whilst formulating my thinking over many years, I've tried all sorts of ways of explaining this second key concept that I have about effective leaders. Because, of course, when I say 'getting out of the way' I don't mean 'being out of the way' or 'being away.' This is at the heart of the principle of vantage points – leveraging these perspectives and the unique position leaders have to enable two aspects of their leadership influence: (1) understanding and inspiring human beings and (2) creating the conditions for collective creative agency in others. By focusing on these two areas and leveraging the vantage points to support this focus, leaders will effectively get out of the way.

We have been conditioned by years of experience to value 'doing' over 'being.' Much of the work within organizations that involves 'doing' is not undertaken by leaders. It is not the job of leaders. Sometimes leaders should do some doing alongside colleagues to enrich their experience and to 'see up close' to support the vantage point of in amongst; however, for the most part, the doing work or the day job of a leader is to leverage their unique vantage points by engaging across all five of these every day. And by leaders using the abovementioned two aspects of their leadership influence, leadership exists as an experience for others (they experience your being-ness of a leader).

If you are a leader and your day job looks like back-to-back meetings, reporting, authorizing and more meetings, then I am so pleased you have picked up this book! There is a much more productive and rewarding day ahead of you tomorrow, and *Part Four* of this book has a handful of really easy and practical yet powerful tools to help you break the cycle and start leveraging your vantage points straight away! (Note: please be honest about what your day looks like today. Whilst intellectually many of us do understand the importance of the role of the leader, our actual day looks much more like the day I describe at the start of this paragraph than we might like to admit.)

There is a wonderful, easy-to-access and digestible piece of research undertaken by the Work Foundation in 2010 that looks at the difference between good and outstanding leaders.[11] I reference this work often. It contains many takeaways that are really helpful when engaging in practical consideration of what getting out of the way actually means (and why it is a positive and productive action a leader can take). One of the nine main findings that the report says differentiates outstanding leaders from good leaders is that they "take deeper breaths and hold them longer."[12] This is a really beautiful way of describing the fact that outstanding leaders know that even when things go wrong, there is sufficient clarity within the organization and the team and sufficient trust that they themselves do not need to be the rescuer in every situation. They realize that the team has everything that it needs and that they, as the leader, will be provided with data, updates and information to enable them to lead at the appropriate time, and to give sufficient space for everyone to continue with their activity.

I always visualize a manufacturing plant when I think of this particular finding. Many was the time when I worked in factories that the production line would go down and would stop. This cost the organization a lot of money every minute it wasn't at optimum capacity. Almost everyone would rush out onto the shop floor from the offices to be at the scene to 'help.' The best leaders I experienced in these situations were the ones who did not do this. Instead, they 'held their breath.' They let the people who needed to diagnose and fix the problem get on with what they were doing, knowing that they were trusted to do so, and those people would report back seeking assistance or decisions as required. It was uncomfortable for those leaders – it felt a little like they were out of control – but it is most efficient to remember that when you have hired and trained the right people, they have clarity about what to do when situations like this arise and they feel ownership about making the decisions they are skilled to make. Who needs the leader hopping up and down next to them whilst you are trying to fix something, asking questions and offering a view (when they are not the expert because they hired you as the expert!)? That is the leader satisfying their own needs rather than the needs of others.

Whilst it may sound counterintuitive, it is critical that leaders can get out of the way. In order to get out of the way, leaders have to be prepared to get personal and deeply understand human beings, how to think and work systemically, and how to think and work up close. It is only then that leaders can optimize the creative and collective agency of others to make progress and move from A to B, which is their primary job.

Chapter 5

UNDERSTANDING AND INSPIRING HUMAN BEINGS

This book is not a biology book and I am not qualified to talk in any depth about physiology, nor is it a book about psychology or neuroscience. I am a practitioner, not a researcher or an expert in any of these fields. However, what I want to summarize in this part of the book is the importance of understanding human beings, because it is only by genuinely seeking to grow our understanding of others and the human condition that we can truly expect to lead other people. Why is this important when we are talking about getting out of the way? Well, just 'being' is one of the most important ways a leader effectively gets out of the way, helps the team to be at their best and supports the clarity that they are providing. One of the ways of being rather than doing is rooted in the leader understanding that how they are and who they are as a leader is all about relationships and understanding human behaviour and interactions. The job of the leader is to effectively know and continually practice their learning and understanding of humans. By generating this continual understanding, the leader's awareness of who they are and how they are has a deep impact upon the performance and integration and ultimately productivity of the team. Being is doing for a leader, when leading in a human context.

I'm not suggesting that leaders need to be educated to great depth about physiology or psychology or any other discipline associated with humans, but I am suggesting that leaders need to have the following:

- An understanding that, as humans, we are connected emotionally and physically, and our feelings are just as much part of our individuality as our fingerprints. A one-size approach does not fit all.
- An ongoing curiosity to grow their learning and stay up to speed with the latest evidence-based research with regard to human performance and team performance. We don't have to do the research or become experts, but we should not leave it to the human resources profession to be reading and up to speed with this knowledge – it is our job too. Evidence-based research published in journals, books, blogs and online resources enables us to gain further insight into what has been proven to make a difference and we can then adjust our own approach to leadership.
- A deep appreciation that what we do, how we behave and who we are has an impact on the people around us and the people who work with us, and it is our responsibility to be aware of that impact. Whether our intention is good or bad, if someone experiences us negatively, we need to know – not so that we can correct them to let them know our intention was good, but to correct ourselves, so that we are experienced in line with our intentions.

- Our access to our unique vantage points is key. All five of them provide us with lots of opportunities to remain in reflection and in conscious observance of what is happening in our teams from many different angles. This means we are better able to test and decide upon the choices we face daily as to where to make an intervention in order to support the team.

HUMANS

Most people are familiar with the stress response – the fight-or-flight response humans have when they experience threat or danger. As a species, we are hardwired to have this response and it is not an active choice. Threat or danger in the past would have been a lion or a sabre-toothed cat chasing us. In those circumstances, the stress response was vital, pumping blood through our veins to enable us to run or fight, and shutting down unnecessary functions in our body such as digestion. The human body is designed for stress. And stress is designed for acute situations where these physiological changes (i.e. increased cortisol and an increased heart rate in order to push more blood and oxygen to our muscles) are used immediately by the body.

But, today, our stress and our threats are rarely of an acute nature. At times they may be, if we are in a dangerous situation and we need to escape, but most modern-day stress is caused by demands such as a high workload, relationship issues and misunderstandings, long commutes and busy days with no space for rest. The exact same physiological response is taking place, but rather than arising in an acute manner, it is a slow, continuous flow. And with no actual physical need to fight or run to use up our physiological responses, our body's balance is compromised with an oversupply of hormones and physiological changes that challenge our mental and physical health over time. This can result in heart disease, diabetes and other chronic health conditions, and certainly is responsible for the rise of mental health issues we see today. In his book *The Stress Solution,* Dr Rangan Chatterjee explains that "the World Health Organization calls stress 'the health epidemic of the twenty-first century.' Up to 80% of all GP consultations are thought to be somehow related to stress."[13]

Understanding how the human body responds to stress and pressure should be in every leader's 101 training and prominent in their awareness. This is because the conditions that every leader creates and the environment that they promote will either cause stress or alleviate stress for people, and therein lies the choice point for each leader. Leadership is not about you. Rather, leadership is about other people and the impact that you as a leader can have on them. The reason you should be educated and interested as a leader is because stress affects productivity. And your primary interest as a leader (aside from the moral case for doing no harm and keeping everyone healthy as fellow human beings) is to engage and inspire individuals and teams to make progress and get the work that needs to be done completed in support of the shared endeavour.

Some stress is actually good – this is 'eustress' ('eu' being a Greek prefix meaning 'good'). We all need some form of motivation and push to enable our physical body to perform and our mental capacity to peak. We can experience stress as too little to do as well as too much to do in terms of workload. *Figure 16* highlights the optimum balance between stress and performance. At this point, the brain senses excitement and starts to respond, causing physiological adaptations in the body. The body then uses up these physiological changes through the activity, either mental or physical, that is required. As a result, the body does not remain in this adapted state and so there is no imbalance or damage to the person's physical or mental health over time.

FIGURE 16: STRESS AND PERFORMANCE

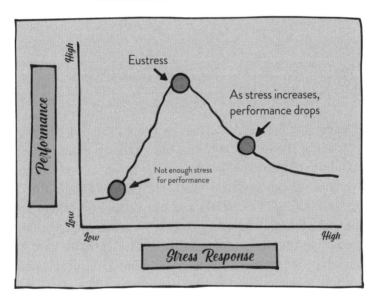

Whilst the working environment is definitely not the only potential cause of overburdensome stress in people, it is, of course, one of the main areas where individuals can experience stress. This situation is further complicated for leaders because no individual will experience stress in the same way or be affected in the same way. Having a good understanding of this human response and understanding how as a leader you can recognize stress in others and how the conditions you set can alleviate this response in others is a lifelong practice. It requires you to be alive to all five vantage points because individual and collective stress can be observed differently from different perspectives. It is critical to be in amongst in two-way dialogue with colleagues. Part of getting out of the way in the human system is to observe and to ask questions in a way that will enable you to best understand what keeps someone in a thriving state and what might tip them into a stressed state.

UNDERSTANDING OURSELVES: BEING HUMAN

If leadership is all about others, why am I starting the 'getting out of the way' part of this book talking about understanding ourselves? The reason is because everything, even our service to others, starts with a deep and unafraid understanding of ourselves and our impact on others. At the end of it all, whatever position we hold, whatever our accountability and responsibility, all we actually have is ourselves. So, we need to understand ourselves deeply and without fear, recognizing our strengths and imperfections, in order to make choices about how we work with our own agency to be in service to others, in leadership.

HUMBLE LEADERSHIP

When I interview for leadership positions, I will often ask the candidate, "Why do you want this position?" or "Why do you want to be a leader/more senior leader?" On the whole, there are two variations on the answer to this question:

VARIATION 1: THE 'I AM REACHING UP' ANSWER. For example, "I feel I am ready for the next step up," "I have been standing in for X manager on plenty of occasions," or "I'd like to take on more responsibility."

VARIATION 2: THE 'TIME SERVED' ANSWER, SOMETIMES CALLED 'ENTITLEMENT' ANSWER. This relies not on leadership ability but a deep understanding of the work of the team or professional field. Examples include "I have been doing this now for many years and am very experienced in this field," and "I believe I have a lot to offer in terms of experience and expertise."

The risk with both of these answers is that they start from 'I' and are about the individual aspiring for recognition, status or the assumed next step on the career ladder. None of these are good reasons for wanting to take on a leadership position or a more senior leadership position. They may be true and they may be part of the story, indeed experience is fantastic and brings a level of perspective and mastery. Striving or reaching for additional responsibility brings a willingness for accountability that is not, in itself, a bad thing. However, when leaders seeks leadership that is about 'I' and not about everyone else, then there is always the risk that ego will mean that the leaders cannot see when they need to get out of the way.

A person who has gained a leadership position for the reasons outlined in variation 1 is at risk of using the resources in the organization to serve their own needs rather than the needs of the business or the wider organization. Because the person is driven by what they believe they are ready for, they become a 'hero' leader and take accountability very seriously; therefore, governance can become overdeveloped and decision-making slow.

A person who has gained a leadership position for the reasons outlined in variation 2 is at risk of not creating sufficient space for their team. The day job of the leader is completely different from the day job of the specialists working in their team. Whilst it is useful and sometimes essential to have this specialist background, without a broader understanding of human dynamics, motivation and inclusive leadership practice, the issue is that all too often there arise layers of hierarchy as 'super-specialists' check up on and duplicate (and often critique) the work of their teams. Creativity is stifled, bureaucracy grows and frustration builds.

There are right reasons for becoming a leader and there are less thoughtful reasons for wanting to be a leader. It all starts, as everything in the human condition does, with a deep understanding and acceptance of oneself regardless of the environment.

The word 'humble' is overused and often we don't spend enough time examining what we really mean by it. For me, the individuals who best lead with humility are those who maintain a spirit of continuous learning and curiosity. They listen to hear, not to reply, and they ask others often. They hold genuine respect for others, even if their views are different. Always choose kindness. Keep a sense of humour, smile often, lift and build others up, and hold yourself lightly. Aiming to keep a focus on these traits keeps us out of judgement and away from the risk of getting in the way. In his 2018 article on this subject in *Forbes*, Jeff Hyman provides a summary of the reasons why humility is an asset in a leader.[14] He references the critically acclaimed *Good to Great* by Jim Collins.[15] In short, it's not about you; it's always about others and the mission. And that is an inside job.

SELF-AWARENESS

We spend all our time with ourselves, and yet I wonder how genuinely self-aware we are. The reason is that we only ever see ourselves from the inside, and this is why the different vantage points are so valuable for leaders to tap into. They help us see ourselves from different perspectives and in different situations, and enable us to understand our impact on others. We may subscribe to the concept of humble leadership as described, but how do we know whether our perception of ourselves as a truly humble leader is the same as that experienced by others?

No doubt you will have been filmed or recorded at some time in your life. I am regularly exposed to such media and I am still always really surprised by how I sound. I just don't sound like that to myself! And don't even get me started on how I look on camera, because the view I see of myself in the mirror is just not the same as the one on the screen. I can recall being filmed for a BBC2 documentary back in 2015, and I could hardly bear to watch it – even through my fingers – because I could not get over the unrecognizable me. However, every single other person watching this documentary commented only on my contribution – what I was saying and doing. They didn't have this veil of shame or disbelief to go through when watching exactly the same thing. There aren't many people who don't find watching or hearing themselves confronting and uncomfortable but, in leadership, facing ourselves is arguably one of the most important practices, and we need to nurture it all the time.

Why? Well, because, as outlined in the introduction to this part of the book, leadership is not about us. It is about others. So, from that perspective we need to intimately care about how others experience us. If there is a gap between our intention and how we are experienced, then we need to do something about it.

How do we grow self-awareness? I cover some tips on this in the toolkit in *Part Four*, so more on that to come, but essentially we need to find ways of seeing ourselves through other people's eyes and ears. And we need to get comfortable with that discomfort. To steer away from this understanding is to fundamentally retain the idea of leadership as an activity that is about ourselves and not about others. The primary goal of leaders is to enable individuals and teams to take action and make progress towards a shared endeavour. And if there is truly a gap between your intention as a leader, which I have to assume for the most part is honourable, and how this is experienced by others, then you suboptimize your ability to perform your role. *Figure 17* outlines the potential gap between our perception of ourselves and our intentions (leftmost circle) and the experience of others (rightmost circle). If there is no gap or minimal gap (as in the right-hand part of the figure), then this is great to know and means that you can continue with much of your practice as it is aligned with others' experience of you.

FIGURE 17: SELF-AWARENESS
– INTENTION VERSUS THE EXPERIENCE OF OTHERS

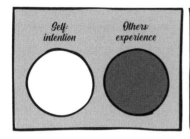
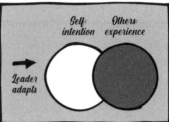

However, if there is a gap (as in the leftmost part of the figure), what do you do? This is a critical aspect of getting out of the way for a leader. *You* are the one who needs to adapt, adjust and change your approach. It is not for others to be told their experience is wrong. It can't be. It is what it is. It is only wrong in the sense that it doesn't match your intention. Always be prepared to listen to feedback in whatever form and from whichever vantage points (use them all!), and always be open to the humble practice of listening and seeking to learn. Don't be entrenched in your way of being; be flexible to adapt to everyone and this will always place you in a strong place in terms of ensuring inclusivity.

Consider how others experience you. For example, do you come across as approachable or aloof? Do you engender a sense of psychological safety where everyone feels they can express themselves or is that not people's experience? Your behaviours and the way you are from day to day create experiences for others that may or may not align with how you see yourself. Moreover, in some organizations, your job level and title will create a sense of distance or gap between your intention and how people experience you

– even if you have never actually met. People will project certain expectations and their own assessment of their own experience of you as a leader, at times solely based on your position. This could be because they associate all people of a certain leadership level with asking challenging questions, for example, or perhaps they don't expect (or want) you to talk to them if they are at a different level in the organization. Is that fair? Certainly not for you as the leader. Is it so? Probably. Be aware of these possibilities and make sure that you are fully open to making the necessary adjustments. How others experience and see you is reality. What you hear and understand in your own head, is the reality of one – yourself. And you need to be willing to see yourself through others' eyes and get comfortable with the discomfort of adjusting for others.

UNDERSTANDING OUR TEAMS

In *Part Two*, we explored some aspects of team creation and team adaptation by 'colouring in.' In this way, we can create clarity around how we resource the work that needs to be done and how we can set expectations such that there is shared clarity between individuals and teams with regard to the work and behaviours that will enable productivity.

From the perspective of getting out of the way, leaders need to understand teams as collections of human beings. A leader who aims only to consider people as a resource – who does not fully understand the multidimensionality of the human experience and how to engage and inspire certain actions and behaviours with adaptation for difference

– is a leader who has perhaps not truly and fully understood the role that they are taking on. Leadership is human, and with that comes all the complexity of understanding individual motivations and group dynamics. So, in this part of our exploration of getting out of the way, we will look at teams from the perspectives of the individual and the team itself. We will also explore a model that I call the 'employee experience investment continuum' – basically, it is about what to consider in terms of investing in team wellbeing and productivity.

THE INDIVIDUAL

In 1960, Douglas McGregor introduced the concepts of Theory X and Theory Y in his book *The Human Side of Enterprise.*[16] In the *Harvard Business Review* paper "Beyond Theory Y," published in 1970, authors John J. Morse and Jay W. Lorsch conducted a study expanding on McGregor's theory. They described his original proposition thus:

1. "Theory X assumes that people dislike work and must be coerced, controlled, and directed towards organizational goals. Furthermore, most people prefer to be treated this way, so they can avoid responsibility."

2. "Theory Y – the integration of goals – emphasizes the average person's intrinsic interest in his work, his desire to be self-directing and to seek responsibility, and his capacity to be creative in solving business problems."[17]

McGregor's theories, along with many of the motivational theories of the 20th century, have been debated and further examined in various organizational settings over many years. Fundamentally, if you subscribe to Theory X, then it is much less likely that you will be able to get out of the way. You will be in a place of high clarity but less empowerment, which in turn has the potential to introduce and exacerbate the individual human stress response and reduce creativity, innovation and self-starting productivity. If leaders are struggling with this concept and feel that the people in their teams are more in the Theory X camp, I encourage them to look at themselves – are they? If so, I'm wondering why they have taken on a leadership role, but I have rarely come across a leader who believes themselves to be a Theory X employee. So why, I would ask them, are you any different from the people who work with you? In my experience, most people, even in some of the most difficult of tasks, are in their hearts more intrinsically motivated to do good work than anything else – if provided with the right encouragement and support. I encourage leaders to read widely on the subject of human motivation from some of the historical studies of the 20th century through to the present day methodologies, in particular in the field of positive psychology.

Martin Seligman is often referred to as the father of positive psychology and reading his work is essential in understanding the evolution of thinking and research into human motivation. An easily accessible first reach into this work is a presentation he gave in 2012, available on YouTube, outlining the principles of positive psychology with his PERMA model.[18] This model outlines the scientifically researched evidence about higher functioning in individuals (children and adults). The PERMA model says that individuals operate in the optimum flourishing or thriving state through the experience of and by focusing on:

- Positive emotion: feeling good and experiencing pleasure
- ·Engagement: absorption in the task or activity to the point of 'flow,' where time seems to stand still
- Relationships: where there is the experience of understanding and respect
- Meaning: a sense of purpose or contribution to something wider than ourselves
- Accomplishment: feeling productive

The key point for leaders is to ensure that there is an understanding of individual motivation and theory and what this means in practice for the relationship between leader and team member. The essence of a leader getting out of the way of an individual (or team) is to ensure that there is sufficient support and space for people to flourish. And flourishing is scientifically proven to be enhanced by the enablement of the above five key aspects of a person's experience. One thing is for sure: whilst there are some overarching common aspects to motivating and enabling people, everyone is different. Leaders who are not curious about educating themselves in this work risk creating obstacles and certainly are at risk of not being able to get out of the way. This is because the essence of getting out of the way has to be a focus on coaching and supporting individuals and/or the team to be independent and self-starting.

In addition to individual human motivation and psychology, the other key field of interest in understanding individuals is in the area of behavioural science. This is a relatively new field of study, rooted in scientific research and neuroscience, but there are some fascinating real-life case studies available that demonstrate the very subtle nuances that make a difference with regard to human behaviour.

I am referring to what is commonly called 'nudge' theory. In their book *Nudge: Improving Decisions about Health, Wealth and Happiness*, Richard H. Thaler and Cass R. Sunstein introduced not only research into how the brain works when it comes to choices presented to humans but also, and critically, ways in which the brain can be moved or nudged in a certain direction with regard to that choice, particularly if the proposition makes the choice easier for them.[19] Understanding this concept and thinking about how to help individuals to make choices that are easy and desirable is a tool in the leader's toolbox when it comes to understanding individual and human behaviour.

Some practical ways to bring these ideas to life in your leadership practice are as follows:

- **BUILD A CULTURE THAT SUPPORTS A PERMA EXPERIENCE.** If you build your communication approach and your being as a leader around the principles of the PERMA model and prioritize the five abovementioned experiences for individuals, the sense of possibility and belonging will be strong. In order to do this, you need to generate a deep interest in the types of strength that individuals have to bring and how they best flourish personally within these different aspects of human experience.

- **GET TALKING AND LISTENING.** As mentioned, the Work Foundation looked into the difference between good and outstanding leaders. The resulting findings highlighted that "talk is work" for leaders.[20] Talking and listening to others is a crucial part of your work as a leader. *Chapter 4* discussed the importance of 'sharing the view' as part of creating clarity, and certainly two-way communication is an aspect of reinforcing the direction and ensuring that there is a shared understanding of expectations. Equally, there is a key element of talking and listening that is very much about the being of the leader. When trying to make a difference as a leader, it is important to listen to hear, be openly curious and leverage all five vantage points – not only seeking to understand different viewpoints but also reflecting with the inside vantage point.

- **ADOPT A COACHING APPROACH.** In *Figure 18* I have tried to very simply visualize the point of coaching as a technique that leaders can use to get out of the way. Coaching predominantly involves listening and asking questions. At times there may be a call for a more directive form of coaching (which may be in service of clarity), but for the most part helping individuals to find their own way encourages ownership and develops more self-sufficiency in that individual in the future (enabling more getting out of the way for leaders). If an individual is working through a problem, or looking to find a way forward with an action, the listening part of coaching provides the conditions for the individual to feel safe to move forward with their own problem-solving and ideas. Moreover, asking the right question (e.g. "I wonder if you have any thoughts on what might work here as a next step?") enables the leader to side-step and clear the path ahead for the individual or team to move into the space themselves. The question is the tool at this point – it literally enables the leader to get out of the way. Just imagine what might happen if you then strengthened this with a slightly deeper question (e.g. "I'd love to hear your thoughts on what might work here as a next step?"). Now not only is the invitation there for the individual to

step into the space, but there is also active encouragement that you are interested in what they have to say.
Further, you build their confidence by showing them
that you believe they know the answer.

FIGURE 18: COACHING AS A MECHANISM FOR GETTING OUT OF THE WAY

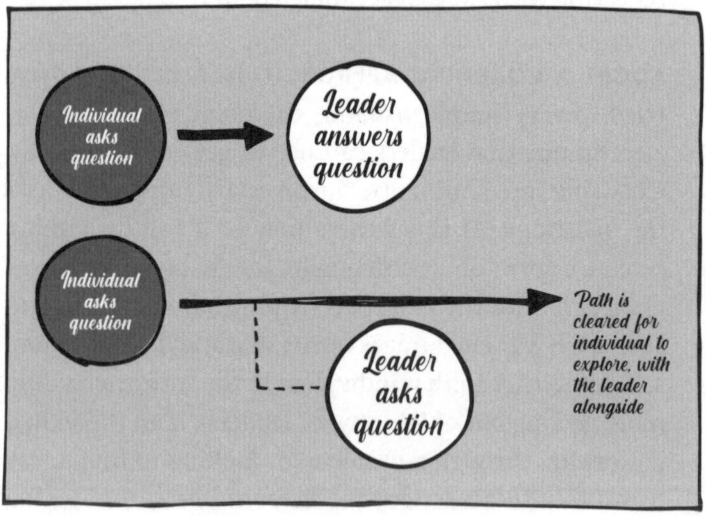

- **NOTICE WHETHER YOU ARE JUDGING.** We are all prone
  to judgement. We experience a situation or a person and,
  based on the paradigms that we are mostly exposed to
  throughout our lives, we make assumptions and evalu-
  ations. Before we know it (and we usually don't notice
  because this happens unconsciously and quickly based
  on our brain referring to patterns that are established
  to help us reduce the amount of processing that it has
  to do for us), we have made a decision about someone
  or something. That might be an assumption about

their intention, what they think or feel, their capability or any other such aspect of our connection with them. As leaders, it is really important to cultivate sufficient understanding and self-awareness to know when we are sitting in judgement and how to move away from it so as to get out of the way of others (and ourselves!). *Figure 19* visualizes the 'ladder of inference,' a model that demonstrates how people can end up way apart from each other by making assumptions and sitting in judgement. It also demonstrates how to revert to curiosity and seek to understand in order to check whether or not our assumptions and judgements are real, valid or fair.

FIGURE 19: THE LADDER OF INFERENCE

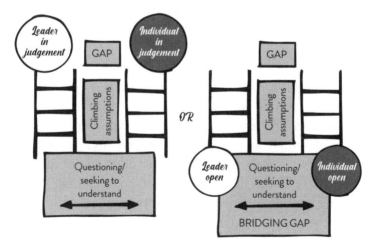

THE EMPLOYEE EXPERIENCE INVESTMENT CONTINUUM

As we have established, as a leader you are primarily concerned with enabling and empowering the people who work with you to perform activities such that they make progress from A to B with whatever it is that defines your shared endeavour. This could be a strategic shift or project, or it could be the high-quality execution of daily operational tasks.

We have also discussed the fact that leadership is not about us, the leaders. It is about others. So how others are experiencing their working environment and whether they have the conditions to thrive is important to us because it will affect their productivity. And we are interested in productivity because that is the activity that will enable us to make the progress from A to B. Therefore, it is imperative that leaders care deeply about creating the conditions required for employees to have experiences that enable them to thrive and perform.

Although this is changing, investment in the wellbeing and emotional health of people in the workplace is still seen as discretionary. It is perceived as something that it might be good to do if we can afford it, but perhaps not a worthy investment, especially as the tangible outcomes of such an investment would be hard to define and describe. When you are considering investments in your organization, it is one of your core responsibilities to think about investing proactively in your employees.

Let's look at *Figure 20*, which shows an employee or team member. There is little doubt that this employee (and indeed any employee) will cost an organization a certain amount of money over time to support their experience. This is not the money it costs to pay them or their benefits – this is to support their experience, wellbeing and engagement. And this figure represents to us that we can spend this money either reactively or proactively in support of the employee's working experience.

FIGURE 20: THE EMPLOYEE EXPERIENCE INVESTMENT CONTINUUM
– STARTING POINT

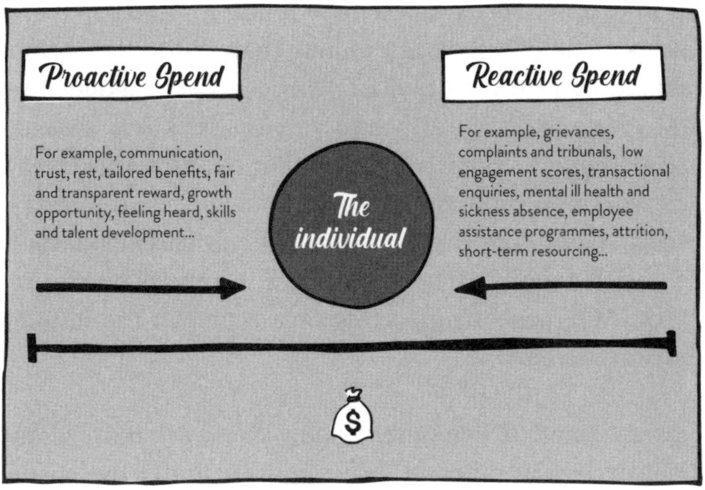

Proactive Spend

For example, communication, trust, rest, tailored benefits, fair and transparent reward, growth opportunity, feeling heard, skills and talent development...

The individual

Reactive Spend

For example, grievances, complaints and tribunals, low engagement scores, transactional enquiries, mental ill health and sickness absence, employee assistance programmes, attrition, short-term resourcing...

The individual is a human being – a human being who breathes, has muscles and organs, and a whole physiology supported by their emotional and mental wellbeing. People are not commodities or resources. They are individuals with a complex operating system that we should be interested in keeping in optimum shape. Individuals have emotions and feelings, all of which can affect their behaviour, their ability to connect with others and their productivity.

The examples in *Figure 20* show how the money we spend on the employee's experience – either reactively or proactively – is spent particularly *because* that individual is a human being.

So as leaders we have a choice about how we want to spend this money. We can consider that investment in wellbeing, clear communications, rest, skills and talent development are discretionary; however, on average this will not reduce the cost. The cost will remain the same. It will just show up in reactive spend and will be found in places like low engagement (which leads to less-than-optimum performance), more transactional enquiries to be responded to and resourced, mental health services, sickness absence and potentially legislative action that requires a response. The cost will show up, however difficult it is to see the linear causal connection – it is difficult to demonstrate this with tangible business cases and return on investment (ROI) papers supporting investment in the human employee experience.

Figures 21 and *22* demonstrate how spend can move along a continuum in different directions. Less proactive spend on the things that make a difference to the employee experience will mean more reactive spend at some point, somewhere else in the organization or in the future. More proactive spend means less reactive spend, reducing the risk of *Figure 20*'s examples of reactive spend arising.

FIGURE 21: THE EMPLOYEE EXPERIENCE INVESTMENT CONTINUUM
– REACTIVE SPEND

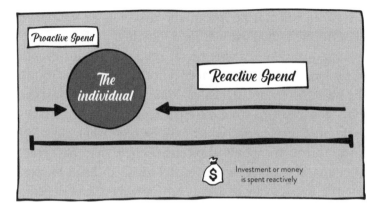

FIGURE 22: THE EMPLOYEE EXPERIENCE INVESTMENT CONTINUUM
– PROACTIVE SPEND

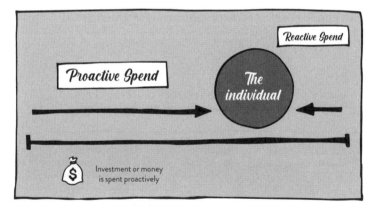

Figure 23 brings this all together to make a final and really critical point: the multiplier effect. This is because the individual pictured (and in real life!) is not a resource but a human being with emotions and feelings and a physiologically balanced body. If we are encountering the types of

interventions and activities associated with reactive spend, the individual will be experiencing a stress response. But the effect will not be linear; the cost will be multiplied because the individual will have lost their enthusiasm for the organization or the team (or the leader) and this will likely have a contagious effect on other employees (think the water cooler or tea breaks). Time will be lost whilst the individual recovers from the emotional impact or indulges their emotional needs, which will be high when they feel under threat. We should also consider here that these reactive situations can be low level and highly difficult to spot, but the impact can be huge. An individual experiencing low-level stress every day because their wellbeing is not being attended to such that they can thrive may show only a small, incremental reduction in productivity. However, that small reduction and contagion to others over time is extremely costly to an organization – a hidden and completely avoidable cost.

FIGURE 23: THE EMPLOYEE EXPERIENCE INVESTMENT CONTINUUM – THE MULTIPLIER EFFECT OF REACTIVE SPEND

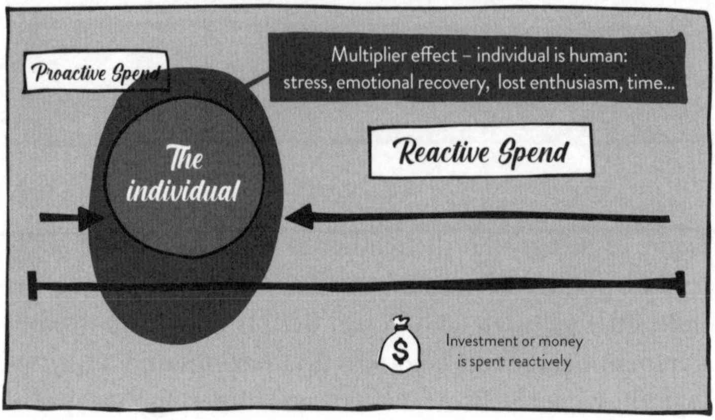

This is where you, the leader, can make a huge difference. You can leverage all your vantage points and consider how best you can create the proactive investment for your employees that enables them to be at their best. It is a very strong visual for getting out of the way as a leader because this isn't about you or your needs. What you need is for your people to be thriving and, to do that, you need to invest in their wellbeing. You will find it difficult to make individual cases for investment in some instances – for example, when you need to convince those who have a sensing preference for data and detail (based on the definitions in the Myers–Briggs Type Indicator relating to a preference for data and objective information rather than intuition).[21] But this is intuitively the right thing to do, so my recommendation is to work with higher-order evidence such as empirical or work-based studies when campaigning for investment in these areas rather than detailed cost analysis or ROI-based approaches. For example, according to *The Sunday Times'* Best Companies to Work For 2020, "Every good employer knows that success begins with an energised workforce and a sense of purpose. Positive workplace cultures give people a sense of fulfilment and motivation, encouraging them to go the extra mile and delight customers."[22]

THE TEAM

It can be amazing when groups of people come together to work on something with purpose and a sense of shared endeavour, and the relationships that people build can forge amazing partnerships where skills are mutually reinforced. A lot of the time, though, when groups of people work together it can be messy, difficult, and fraught with misunderstanding and conflict. For leaders, far from being able to get out of the way, they may feel drawn into solving, mediating and making decisions because the team members are unable or ill-equipped to make those decisions collectively. When a leader plays this role, it becomes self-reinforcing as a way of working as the team defers to the leader for all decisions and relies on that deep engagement for effective working and conflict resolution. It may not be possible for leaders to step back all of the time, and sometimes it is most helpful and expedient for them to step in to mediate or make a decision. However, leaders must have the awareness to notice how often this is happening and whether stepping in too often creates passivity and reliance in the team and therefore a reluctance to work together to solve problems. A leader who is regularly drawn into mediation and problem-solving is less able to find the time and space themselves to continue to see the big picture via all vantage points – they find themselves predominantly in amongst.

There isn't an easy answer or any magic wand that you can wave to optimize the way people work together. You need to remain curious and open to learning all the time to spot patterns of behaviour in yourself and your team, and to create the conditions for effective working. The vantage points are helpful when it comes to group dynamics and group working because they enable you to spot opportunities and problems early and to create clarity, which is one of the key issues relating to effective teamwork.

Every organization or team I have worked in has had crises. Something happened and everyone had to put their shoulder to the wheel to make things go. Inevitably, in such cases, everyone reflects afterwards on how brilliantly the team cooperated and says things like, "Isn't it incredible how we work so well in a crisis?" and "Why can't we work so well all the time?" During a crisis, teams collaborate cross-functionally, share information, get things done and make decisions. People trust one another to deliver their part and not interfere as they are too focused on delivering their own aspects of the work. But once this interesting observation of how well the team can work in a crisis is concluded and a little time has passed, nothing changes, and it is forgotten until the next crisis, which inevitably comes.

Whilst it is in no one's interest to be permanently in crisis, the interdependency between the two jobs of a leader – creating clarity and getting out of the way – is exemplified in these situations. Crisis always creates clarity. There is usually a very straightforward and clear decision to be made, a direction is provided, everyone faces towards it together, and that sense of shared endeavour foregrounds the traits of cooperation and information-sharing. So point number one about effective group dynamics and the leader's role is actually nothing to do with getting out of the way and all about creating the parameters of clarity. We discussed this in *Part Two*.

There has been much research and writing about high-performing teams and the role of the leader. Whilst it would be difficult to pick one reference (or the two or three key aspects of this body of thought), my main message here to leaders is to do the reading and research. Constantly being curious about team-working and team dynamics is the key to successful leadership. If you are interested in building the most effective team possible, probably the most seminal work (and the most easily digestible, as it is written as a series of fables) is Patrick Lencioni's *The Five Dysfunctions of a Team*,[23] which effectively lays out step-by-step requirements for team effectiveness. However, to begin looking at the thinking around how you can get out of the way with regard to group dynamics and harnessing the very best of teams, here are some thought-starters to help you build your practice (and it is a practice – you will be constantly evolving the way you support teams throughout your leadership journey):

- **BE CLEAR.** As explained in *Part Two* and reiterated in this chapter, clarity creates shared endeavour and will help to head off at the pass many issues that arise in ineffective team and group behaviour. Bringing people into that creation of clarity is a key element of creating an effective team. By providing some structure but helping teams to be part of defining the direction and giving them access to your vantage point as a leader so they themselves can own the direction collectively and up front, you will enable them to ensure they are interpreting that direction collectively in the same way. This allows people to listen and raise challenges so as to reach a shared understanding. Even if the direction doesn't always match everyone's preferences, they will feel heard and involved and will have every opportunity to understand the 'why.'

- **BE FAIR AND INCLUSIVE.** We want diverse teams – a collection of people with different backgrounds and perspectives to help us notice a much wider spectrum of opportunities and risks than we might if we were all looking through the same lens. We want everyone's strengths, and we acknowledge, therefore, that there will be areas that some are not as strong in. That is the team. So, use the vantage points of from high above and to the side and around to step away in order to observe and see the opportunities for wider inclusion at all times.

- **CONFLICT IS OK.** We have an idea that a team of people need to be in harmony for high performance. However, we know from much research that this is not actually the case; higher-performing teams have the ability to disagree, which creates an environment of optimum improvement all the time. What this requires, however, is for you as the leader to create conditions that promote psychological safety. In these conditions, team members can bring their authentic perspectives together in a respectful and dynamic way. In her 1999 paper "Psychological Safety and Learning Behavior in Work Teams," Amy Edmondson describes psychological safety as "a shared belief held by members of a team that the team is safe for interpersonal risk taking."[24] This paper and countless other research studies and publications articulate the same phenomenon around effective teams. This is that individuals need to feel that it is safe and that they will not be penalized in any way for expressing their views and feedback freely, even if they differ from the majority. If we want to optimize diversity in teams and get the best from our creative problem-solving, then this needs to be attended to. And it all stems from the leader. It is about who the leader is and how they behave when receiving feedback or a different view from the one they or the majority of others hold. Leaders need to actively demonstrate respect and gratitude for a wide range of perspectives and contributions, and actively demonstrate that learning mindset. Not only will the team benefit from these conditions so creativity and problem-solving can flourish, but also risks are much more likely to be identified early, enabling action to be taken (rather than people hiding their issues for fear that they will be blamed or there will be some sort of personal repercussion). As a leader, it is not so much about what you say with regard to creating psychological safety for your team and organization – it is much more about what you do. Practise a calm approach, take a breath so you don't respond immediately without controlling your emotions and don't shoot the messenger if there is difficult news to hear!

- **CELEBRATE THE TEAM.** Take sufficient time exploring your different vantage points such that you are regularly aware of the milestones and contributions that require celebration. Put in place ways in which you and your team can reflect and recognize great contributions. By leveraging your different vantage points, be sure to keep an eye out for everyone, not just the people in your closer network, so the team is fully inclusive. Praise the everyday and the activities that demonstrate the values of consistent strong performance, which does a lot to prevent crisis. Occasionally, heroics in a team do require recognition, but not all the time. The more the collective shares in social interaction and good feelings together, the more connected they will feel and the more attracted they will be to the shared vision and endeavour.

- **INVEST IN THE TEAM.** Part of getting out of the way for the leader is getting out of the way of the day-to-day productive work of the team and regularly investing time in its dynamics. A plant doesn't grow without light and water, and it is the leader's job to provide that light and water to the team. In a group of humans, there is always a need to provide space to talk, to create and reinforce social connections and bonds, and to build shared understanding.

- **IT IS THE 'TOGETHER' THAT CREATES THE POWER.** Individual superstars are fantastic but, in most teams, it is the collaboration and support that they give each other to work together and help each other that create high performance. Groups of superstars often underperform because they are less used to collaborating and, as such, they are focused on their own individual achievement. Therefore, the key is to build what is often called 'social capital' – the bonds between people where conflict can exist and lead to respectful challenge, and where everyone is looking out for each other and not allowing anyone else to fall behind. In her 2015 TED Talk "Forget the Pecking Order at Work," Margaret Heffernan discusses this very concept.[25] Teams work best when the collective nature is nurtured. Therefore, as a leader, hire for collaboration and connection, not individual performance.

UNDERSTANDING OUR HUMAN ORGANIZATION AND WIDER ENVIRONMENT

From the vantage points of from high above and from high out and beyond, leaders have the possibility of seeing broader perspectives and contextualizing these for the team. This helps with setting the scene in terms of clarity. In terms of getting out of the way, one of the jobs of the leader is to ensure that whilst the team is delivering, the leader is creating a relationship between what the team is doing and the rest of the wider organization, system or industry (for example). This may take the form of communicating data, progress, new innovations or ways of working to key stakeholders, or it may mean bringing outside perspectives back to the team and ensuring that there is an ongoing dialogue and communication mechanism that plugs the work of the team in to other humans in other parts of the organization and system. As such, there is an opportunity to create further connections and to monitor how those connections are working in (e.g. there might be a need to modify something that the team is doing in order to fit with a change elsewhere in the organization or to build relationships cross-functionally to ensure that handoffs between functions or teams are effective).

The leader doesn't have to do all of this (although there may be some aspects that they need to support), but they certainly need to be leveraging their vantage points to ensure that this is happening in the most effective way, taking into account not only the task but the relationships as well.

We will explore the concept of seeing things systemically in *Chapter 6* in a little more detail. However, from the perspective of the human being and the leader, human systems and wider contexts are ever changing and complex. They require us to leverage the vantage points available to us to bring news of other 'tribes' and share our messaging to ensure there is clarity, understanding and collaboration, always seeking to understand and relate to that wider perspective.

ONE THING YOU COULD DO WITH EACH VANTAGE POINT WHEN UNDERSTANDING HUMAN BEINGS

IN AMONGST. It may be obvious, but listening and talking are the opportunity when in amongst. As human leaders of human beings, we should take every opportunity to connect. I always remember that when I worked at the world headquarters of the Ford Motor Company, the then CEO, Bill Ford, had lunch in the canteen every day along with everyone else. He was visible and everyone could see him filling up his tray and paying for his lunch like everyone else, which helped others to see him as a fellow human. People would feel they could approach him and talk to him – maybe just small talk, but that relationship capital, built up in small moments, was valuable in the bigger moments. Social relationships are built on reciprocity: I share something about me, so you are likely to share something about you and we build trust and rapport. As a leader, I want people to feel trusted because they are then likely to feel more free to contribute to their full creative potential. I also want to be trusted that I have their and the organization's best interests at heart as I make decisions. They will also be more likely to buy in to the direction I work with them to set.

TO THE SIDE AND AROUND. From a team dynamics perspective, you are going to want to leverage this vantage point to enable you to understand the relationships and effectiveness of your teams. If you are in amongst with a team, it is likely that the dynamics will be altered simply because of your presence. Have you ever been part of a team when the leader joined a team meeting? The person who is usually on their phone not listening will suddenly be attentive. The person who talks over other people may do this less. Suddenly everyone is there, when usually there are a couple of people who can't make the meeting because they have another priority. So there is a limitation to in amongst because people change their behaviour around you. However, you can understand team dynamics by observing to the side and around – for example, by gathering survey data about the team, or even encouraging the team to use data such as psychometrics to understand preference and difference (this will also enable you to see whether the make-up of the team is skewed in any way towards a particular characteristic). Another way to observe is to provide the team with a challenge or a particular task or objective, and encourage them to solve the problem, reporting back to you not only on the outcome of the task but also on how they felt they worked together and what could have been improved or might have worked better.

FROM HIGH ABOVE. From this vantage point, one of the obvious opportunities is to conduct surveys and questionnaires in order to gather systemic and holistic data about the engagement and wellbeing of the team. This enables you to learn more about the feelings, motivations and experiences of the team or organization and, therefore, to understand whether there are any areas where interventions may be required. The challenge with surveys is that they may be seen as creating a manager – employee divide, because the employee fills it in and hands it over to management to do something with the results. The manager can feel there are a host of requirements, requests and even complaints to which they cannot or do not have the answer. Sometimes surveys are run and then teams discuss them and create lovely action plans that rarely actually make a difference. My preference if you are really going to get out of the way as a leader is to approach surveys about engagement and wellbeing from a shared ownership perspective. A leader cannot engage anyone. Individuals have to engage themselves. What a leader can do is facilitate an honest discussion that opens up communication and joint problem-solving, which is shared between the leader and the team or individual. This is survey-gathering as a human leadership approach, rather than a task-based approach. And the data will be liberating and insightful for everyone.

FROM HIGH OUT AND BEYOND. A leader who is really curious about human beings will constantly want to learn and grow their understanding. I say this firstly because leadership is a practice, so we are never the finished article. But, secondly, I point this out because our understanding of ourselves as humans is evolving all the time. Neuroscience and studies looking at how our minds and our physicality work are providing us with gifts of insight every year as more and more discoveries are made. This will help us all to better understand our mental health, our physical health, and how to thrive and be together. Spending time in the from high out and beyond vantage point when understanding humans is learning.

INSIDE. Following on from the previous point, spending time inside is learning. It is learning about ourselves and applying our insights to our own practice such that we continue to delve deeper into self-awareness and understanding of our impact on others (leadership is about others, but it starts with an understanding of ourselves). I highly recommend that leaders regularly take a psychometric test or a leadership diagnostic test and work with a coach to help them explore this learning, keep growing and keep evolving their understanding. Self-awareness is necessary as it leads to self-care and compassion, which are critical if we want to lead other humans with being-ness that lifts them up to shared and collective agency.

Chapter 6

CREATING THE CONDITIONS FOR COLLECTIVE AGENCY IN OTHERS

The job of the leader is to create clarity and get out of the way, and the primary purpose of this is to enable individuals and teams to actively pursue and deliver progress in moving from A to B. Given that this is the critical purpose, the concluding chapter of this exploration of the concept of getting out of the way considers the leader's role in creating the right conditions for generating collective agency in others (for them to get from A to B).

The starting point is the creation of clarity and continually working towards clarity with others. This creates the parameters and the destination – if you like, the broad pathways that we want to collectively travel along. The leader has the tools discussed in *Part Two* to create this clarity: setting the scene, colouring in (which includes resourcing the work and setting expectations) and sharing the view.

By getting out of the way, the leader fulfils their role of enablement – that is to say, creating self-sufficiency within their team to enable its members to make progress within the parameters and towards the direction as set out by establishing and building clarity. This is only achieved by the leader understanding humans (including themselves, individuals and team dynamics) as well as seeing things systemically and up close.

I encourage you to reflect upon the development of collective agency in others as the main objective of any leader. So, however you choose to get there – however much emphasis you place on each of the different aspects we have discussed in this book so far – your objective is to enable others to move from A to B through their own collective agency.

Often, I hear analogies in business referring to boats, such as 'it takes a long time to turn a supertanker around.' I'm going to jump on the bandwagon here and add in the visualization of a large rowing vessel. A leader in this situation cannot possibly row the boat themselves. Firstly, oars need to move through the water on both sides to propel the boat forwards in a straight line – if the boat were only rowed on one side, it would simply move in circles. Secondly, everyone needs to row in unison otherwise the oars would crash together, the boat would lose momentum (it might move, but not efficiently or smoothly), people would get frustrated, and there would be confusion and little harmony. What is necessary is clarity of direction – for example, we are going to row to that island and land in that small harbour. If everyone transparently knows what they are doing, the crew can make adjustments by steering themselves along the way as well as being guided. In addition, knowing why they are going to that particular harbour (e.g. to pick up supplies) will create motivation to work hard. Finally, having the right people with the right skills on board means the vessel will be resourced appropriately, and agreeing expectations will mean that they all know what they need to do as individuals and as a team (and they will be able to express what they need from a leadership role).

The leader in this situation, on the basis of this clarity, is able to access all five vantage points to observe and gather information and to provide support to the team without getting in the way. The leader is essentially another role in the team, enabling the performance of the individuals and the collective group. There will be moments on the voyage when the leader might need to provide in amongst support (e.g. someone injures their arm and decisions need to be made about whether to replace that individual or rest for a time). However, there will also be moments when the vessel is moving in the right direction, smoothly and harmoniously, and the leader can look to the horizon, scan for weather changes (for example), and create the appropriate connections between that information and the crew on the boat. Or they can think ahead to the arrival at the harbour and what might be required at that point. Think back to *Figure 2*, which provides an overview of the jobs a leader has (to create clarity and get out of the way), which are supported by the leader's unique vantage points, which can all be used for the purpose of creating collective agency in others so they can get from A to B.

This analogy outlines the simplicity of leaders creating clarity and getting out of the way. A leader needs to be fully and consciously focused on the purpose of their role. Leadership is not about you; it is about others. And, essentially, it is about supporting and enabling others to make progress in moving from A to B with as much self-sufficiency as possible. I often find that leaders do not express the outcome of their role and their work in this way. Often leaders will express the outcome of their role in a 'doing' sense: for example, we need to achieve growth of 6% next year in our profit or we need to introduce this new product or we need to deliver this technology upgrade to our business. These are all quite possibly true statements and they can help to provide part of the clarity needed by the team and organization. They are descriptions of the 'where' part of scene-setting (see *Chapter 2*). But they are not descriptions of the outcome the leader needs to achieve in order to fulfil these objectives. The leader's job is not the objective itself. The leader's job is to create the collective agency in others to achieve the objectives together. And that is the topic of the tasks and examples I have described in this book. I encourage all leaders to think carefully and consciously about the purpose of the leader. And then do and be that. *Figure 24* demonstrates the difference between a situation where a team support their leader to achieve delivery versus a situation where the leader supports the team to achieve delivery. Leadership is not about you, and your contribution to the shared endeavour is to leverage your vantage points in service of the two jobs that you have to do to support the team: create clarity and get out of the way.

FIGURE 24: TEAM SUPPORTING LEADER VS. LEADER ENABLING TEAM

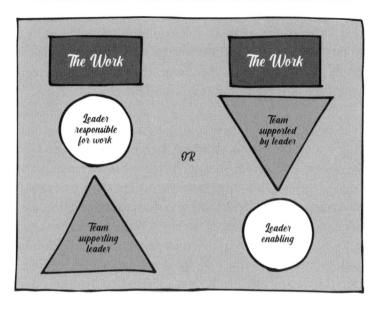

SEEING THINGS SYSTEMICALLY

Everything is connected, whether it is to a wider functional organization, a broader professional discipline, distributed geographies, technological advancement, competition, global political or social changes, etc. The role of the leader is to effectively operate a regular 'scan and connect' activity, which involves moving away from the direct work and activities of the team, and ensuring that there is sufficient attention given to these connections. If the leader is not doing this, then who is?

Some leaders create a strategy function whose role it is to work on these connections. But just as it can be problematic to create a team with responsibility for culture in an organization, delegating strategy is dangerous for leaders. Strategy and culture are the job of the leader. Other people may support the analysis and communications and help to put into practice effective connections, but every leader needs to have a cultivated point of view about the strategic landscape of their area of responsibility.

One of the key practices a leader can employ when getting out of the way is thinking systemically. In *The Fifth Discipline*, MIT senior lecturer Peter Senge articulates the concept of 'systems thinking' by introducing a practice of observing and understanding connections and interdependencies within a larger system.[26] There are perhaps two key ways a leader can enable their team or organization by getting out of the way and thinking and seeing systemically: scanning effectively, and creating connections and plugging in.

SCANNING EFFECTIVELY

One of the ways that a leader gets out of the way is to spend time scanning the wider organization and context. This essentially involves understanding the interdependencies between different moving parts of the wider system and understanding what is moving, changing and happening elsewhere that will have an impact upon the work and activity of the team and vice versa. Because there could be infinite possibilities and connections here, it is crucial for leaders to build the skills of scanning effectively and making choices about the most important and critical aspects of data and information. It is likely that as a leader (probably with a certain industry or professional background) you will scan automatically due to the networks that you engage with and belong to and the publications that you read. One key invitation for leaders is to constantly be aware of the places where it is easier to go for information and insight, and to challenge themselves regularly to gather information from a new or different source, to ensure that there is true diversity. One of the key risks of scanning without this regular challenge in place is that we may find ourselves in a form of 'echo chamber' where we scan only familiar sources that reinforce what we already think, rather than extending ourselves to less comfortable and less obvious sources of information. It is those cross-network references and those different sources in the environment and the wider organization that will identify that efficiency which no one else has seen yet, or identify that product offering which fuses two unlikely elements together and creates a compelling customer proposition.

The key risks with scanning are either that it doesn't happen because it is a strategic venture that there isn't enough time for because there is so much delivery and 'doing' to prioritize, or that it happens only in familiar places within a familiar network. Scanning the environment and looking for those connections and important trends and perspectives is uniquely the role of the leader. They have the necessary vantage points to enable them not only to gather information and inputs from the wider organization or environment but also to turn what they have gathered into clarity and action by doing something with it.

CREATING CONNECTIONS AND PLUGGING IN

As outlined above, leaders get out of the way and create a sense of agency with regard to systemic thinking by doing something with the information and input that they gather. Practically speaking, what this means is that they actively seek out ways in which the team or organization needs to connect with and join up with other parts of the wider system or organization with a two-way flow of information and collaboration. This essentially means building on the interdependencies identified via scanning to determine how to create effective channels of communication and broader understanding, and what those channels should be. For example, if a leader notices other organizations using technology to improve a certain aspect of the customer experience, they might create the appropriate connections between their team and organization and this information and then practise with a view to learning or building a relevant response for their own customers. Or, in another example, a leader might develop a perspective through reading some evidence-based research that provides insight into an emerging field of study. By bringing this insight on the bigger picture to the attention of those in the organiza-tion such that further exploration can take place, the leader may be able to help support an evidence-based review of a certain current practice.

Figure 25 provides a very high-level view of the role of the leader when scanning and creating connections. In terms of seeing things systemically, the leader's value lies in cre-ating the relationship between the scanning and the plug-ging in.

FIGURE 25: SCANNING AND CREATING CONNECTIONS

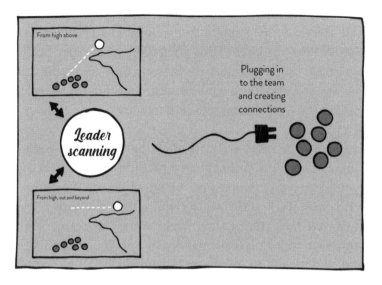

SEEING THINGS UP CLOSE

Whilst seeing things up close could be considered as the opposite of seeing things systemically, this would be a misunderstanding of the role of the leader when leveraging the vantage points of in amongst and to the side and around. In actual fact, using the vantage points and being close to the work and activity of the team are only valuable to leaders when approached with a systemic mindset and a clear intention to be up close for the purposes of creating clarity and getting out of the way. If the leader's intention is to be up close for any other reason than to support these two key jobs, then there is a very real risk that the leader will miss out on the opportunity to support and enable the creativity and self-sufficiency of the team and individuals.

Part Two discussed many of the ways in which a leader can leverage the vantage points of in amongst and to the side and around to help create and support clarity and direction. For the purposes of this discussion, we are specifically looking at how a leader can both be up close and get out of the way. It seems like it could be a paradox. But the solution is all in the focus: being rather than doing.

One way to think about this might be to imagine leadership as a presence rather than a physical reality. So those around you experience your being whilst they continue with their work and their activities, and as a leader you may well take time to 'get back to the floor' and work alongside colleagues to further develop your experience and understanding of the roles and reality of the work and the feelings and relationships between individuals and teams. The key to presence rather than physicality is to recall that leadership is about others. So, in this sense, getting out of the way means recognizing that your presence in amongst and to the side and around is only about information-gathering and fuelling this vantage point such that you are better equipped to do the work of creating clarity.

This is really difficult for leaders. I recognize this and have seen it many times and experienced it myself. When I used to work in factories and a senior leader would come for a visit, the staff would literally repaint a walkway through the plant (it was even called 'the royal route'). The senior leader didn't use the bathrooms that everyone else used (which were not the best) and instead used ones that were more presentable. And they were guided around the bits of the operation that the staff wanted them to see (and that they thought they wanted to see). None of this is of any use for a senior leader, although I must confess that I do think some of them very much enjoyed it (perhaps because the experience was more about themselves than about others). However, there were certainly some leaders who absolutely knew that they were being presented with a glossy cover and would find ways of veering off the route, talking to the people who were not positioned in the right places (designated and briefed to talk to them) and sitting in the staff canteen eating the same lunch as everyone else. There are many forces at work aiming to prevent you as the leader from seeing things up close as they really are. Therefore, the job of getting out of the way and creating the conditions for transparency is absolutely critical.

The opportunity provided to leaders from being up close is not only about creating clarity (and to do that usefully and well, you need to know how things actually are, not how others are presenting them to you). Being up close is about demonstrating that you are out of the way, and this is the key point about being. It is also about what other people need you to be, not what you need to be (leadership is about others' experience of you).

One of the key jobs of a leader is to enable – to look carefully across individuals and teams and to seek out the information that reveals where the leader can create support to enable individuals and teams to thrive. This is based on the premise that the leader has hired the right people, there is a shared endeavour and purpose, and the leader believes that the individuals are all intrinsically motivated to do a good job. There are some behaviours that are key to implementing better teams, including:

- **WHEN SOMETHING ISN'T WORKING SO WELL, ASK WHAT HELP OR SUPPORT IS NEEDED.** There is no blame. Ever. Even if someone makes a mistake. There might be an acknowledgement that things could have been done better, but the immediate question is to ask what help or support is needed. The emphasis here is on the speed of the movement to support and help. That doesn't mean that individuals and teams might not be held to account for critical failures, gross misconduct, or other such serious breaches of contract or trust. However, for the most part these are rare and in these instances swift and private action can be taken as appropriate. Generally speaking, self-starting, creative and innovative teams are those where learning and support are the leadership interventions of choice.

- **ASK WHAT HELP OR SUPPORT IS NEEDED EVEN WHEN THINGS ARE WORKING WELL.** The key role of the leader as an enabler is to ensure that individuals and teams have everything they need to perform their tasks and activities and to feel a sense of belonging and engagement.

- **LISTEN – REALLY LISTEN.** A leader who is genuinely curious and who really wants to make good use of their time up close will ask questions and really listen as much as possible. Seek the opinions of a wide range of people, including as many voices as possible, listening with your ears, eyes and all senses and making notes so you can remember and reflect upon your observations.

- **SHARE INFORMATION TRANSPARENTLY.** The being-ness of a leader talking, imparting information, communicating or sharing insight is in the way in which this happens.

Critically, a leader who is really conscious of the opportunity to ensure that this 'sharing the view' is heard will be looking for signs that what they are communicating has been heard and is understood. It is important to have open Q&As and opportunities to hear back from participants in an open format whilst up close. Whilst this might at times feel uncomfortable, the leader will be available for these purposes because leadership is about others. In addition to practising being-ness, leaders must be willing to be vulnerable. For example, say a question is asked to which the leader doesn't know the answer. It may be that they don't know the answer (leaders don't know everything – check out 'Teacher's trick' in the toolbox coming up in *Part Four*). Alternatively, perhaps the answer is genuinely confidential, in which case share that with the team. Everyone is an adult – people understand and it will build trust if you share that "I can say this much, but at the moment I am afraid I can't say too much more but I will do when I can."

- **CONNECT.** By practising the being-ness of empathy and reciprocity and by establishing connection, leaders will build trust. This, in turn, will create opportunities to grow relationships in which when the leader is up close, people will feel comfortable sharing reality, asking for help and sharing successes. This is about leaders smiling alongside their teams, crying alongside their teams and leaning in to uncomfortable conversations whilst not feeling that they need to have the solution – just being there when someone needs space. These are all aspects of emotional intelligence. In his book of that title, Daniel Kahneman provides extensive research and structure around the relational and human connectiveness that are so important for leaders to creative thriving and flourishing communities working together to achieve outcomes and make progress.[27]

- **CELEBRATE AND RECOGNIZE.** Leaders should positively reinforce great practice and good work, highlighting the connection between what people are doing and how they are being, and why this matters for the clarity and purpose of the organization. You might think that as a leader you do this well. Do it more. Use more effusive language. Smile. Tell people what specifically is so great about their contribution. Leave them skipping home that particular evening because they were *seen* – enabling people to feel seen and heard for their engagement and contribution is one of the most powerful tools a leader has. Get out of the way by truly seeing people.

- **TAKE EVERYTHING BACK TO THE NEST.** I use this analogy because leaders need to be a little bit like birds when leveraging their vantage points. In their practice of getting out of the way, they are effectively flying high in the sky and seeking out sticks with which to build a nest. The importance is twofold here. Firstly, during all the activity that a leader is involved in, they have been out of the way sufficiently to be able to see where clarity is required in terms of support, resources, change of direction or any other such intervention. But all this requires reflection – testing the up-close observations with the whole range of vantage points (including, critically, the vantage point of inside, which enables leaders to take time to reflect). The second important point relates to the transparency with which the leader takes the observations back to the nest. This is key, as others need to be able to see that what the leader observed is being followed up on and built into the wider perspective. This, in turn, builds a stronger connection between individuals and fosters their sense of importance and belonging. Equally, it also helps to build a sense of joint and shared endeavour amongst the team and between individual, team and leader. There is very little that a leader does not need to be fully transparent about.

ONE THING YOU COULD DO WITH EACH VANTAGE POINT WHEN CREATING COLLECTIVE AGENCY

Seeing things up close resides in amongst and to the side and around.

IN AMONGST. This vantage point is where you can experience the energy of a team or organization. When you are in amongst and talking, listening and working alongside, you will be able to sense whether the team and individuals have effective collective agency. You also have the ability to switch from getting out of the way to providing clarity in order to introduce more communications – for example, if greater direction is required. In addition, when you are in amongst, aspects such as recognition and reinforcement can happen in real time to support where collective agency is thriving.

TO THE SIDE AND AROUND. By using performance data as well as metrics that can be seen and gathered up close and alongside the team (and for comparison with other teams and organizations), you will be able to see whether the team is performing optimally or not and making progress in moving from A to B, which is the whole purpose.

Seeing things systemically resides in from high above and from high out and beyond.

FROM HIGH ABOVE. The from high above vantage point allows you to look at the progress of the team or organization. As discussed previously, data metrics such as RAG (red, amber and green) ratings against key performance indicators are useful to help you consider where interventions or direction are required. This vantage point is helpful as it is objective and is based on providing support and enabling others.

FROM HIGH OUT AND BEYOND. This vantage point is helpful for context. It will often enable you to consider the performance and movement of the team against comparators and to consider opportunities for efficiencies, greater collaboration, more teamworking and coordination, and better ways of motivating performance. Seeing things systemically resides in from high above and from high out and beyond.

INSIDE. A leader can truly get out of the way when the team is enabled with clarity to form the best possible collective agency. Things are constantly changing, but it is unlikely that the leaderless team will be commonplace any time soon. There are examples of self-directed teams, but, on the whole, leaders help by providing a focal point for the clarification that enables teams to rise up and thrive. However, in those moments when the team is fully working as a collective towards a clear direction efficiently and effectively, the job of the leader when inside is to rest and recharge, ready to be available to support the team again and work with them to build the shared endeavour.

PART FOUR

Practical Advice

Chapter 7

PRACTICAL TOOLS
FOR LEADERS

In this part of the book, I bring together some of my more commonly used practical tools. I have often used these for myself and others when reflecting on and trying to improve leadership practice. I hope that you find something here with practical relevance that you can use to help you continue to strive to be the best leader that you can be. These are my 12 tools to help you bring clarity to your leadership, get out of the way, and access and make the most of the vantage points that you have as a leader. Some of these tools may speak to you more than others. Use those. Others may be helpful to you later, or you may find you share them with someone else in a coaching format. This is not a checklist of things you should be doing – rather, it is a library of 12 resources that you can dip in and out of and use however you think they will help.

DIARY CHECK

Most of us organize our time through some form of sched-uler, be that an online calendar, a written diary or even just a scheme in our heads. We have some sense of what we have done and what we have coming up. In my experience, the diaries of leaders (and I include myself in this) are often dominated by scheduled meetings, many of which are not scheduled by us. If we are not careful, we move through our days, weeks and months reacting to the diary commitments that we have in place, often lamenting that we don't have time to get the real work done! Often many of our truly important tasks and responsibilities are not part of our schedule and so we miss them, or end up working outside reasonable hours trying to fit in the things we didn't have time to do during the working day.

This does not have to be the case, and the diary check is a very simple and straightforward way to be intentional about your leadership.

In this book, I have outlined the two main responsibili-ties of a leader: to create clarity and to get out of the way. Within these, there are seven aspects of leadership that I suggest you ensure are in place in your practice. The diary check is a two-step exercise (with an optional third step). You will need seven different-coloured highlighter pens or something similar.

STEP 1: REFLECTION

Take your diary from the past two months and print it out so that you can lay it out in front of you (you could use a longer period, but I would suggest two months as a minimum time frame).

The seven aspects of leadership I have outlined in this book are:

1. Setting the scene
2. Colouring in
3. Communicating and comprehension
4. Human beings
5. Seeing things systemically
6. Seeing things up close
7. Creating collective agency in others

Work through every item in your schedule (including unscheduled time where no meetings are present) and highlight each item with a colour representing which area of focus this item in your schedule most closely represents. If items in your schedule do not represent any of the seven areas of focus, this is fine – simply do not highlight them. If an item might represent multiple aspects, just pick the predominant one for this exercise.

Visually, you should now be able to see how much time you have spent on each of these areas in the past two months. There is no right or wrong outcome. Rather, this is an opportunity to visually see how you are spending your time and decide whether there is anything you can learn or change moving forwards.

If you have an area of focus with no highlights, this will offer you an opportunity to reflect on whether you should be doing this activity more.

If you have an area of focus with an overabundance of colour compared to other aspects, this may offer you an opportunity to reflect on whether you should be doing this activity less.

You will undoubtedly have many items in your schedule with no highlighted colour. That is to be expected – our schedules will not be fully composed of our leadership areas of focus, and we will need to attend to others' needs and aspects of governance within our organization. However, consider whether you should be using these unhighlighted meetings and items in your schedule more intentionally and purposefully to fulfil some of the seven aspects. Can you use these as opportunities to move between your five vantage points more readily and change your perspective to create greater leadership value for yourself and your team? With greater clarity, you should be able to start to mine every scheduled and unscheduled opportunity to implement one of the seven aspects of leadership.

STEP 2: THE FORWARDS LOOK

Take your diary for the coming two months and again print it out so that you can lay it out in front of you (you could use a longer period, but I would suggest two months as a minimum time frame).

Again, take your highlighters, one colour for each of the seven aspects of leadership, and highlight every item in your schedule to represent each of those aspects.

Now get to work deciding whether you want to make any changes to your upcoming schedule to make sure that you do not miss any of the key areas of focus. Can you delegate more to get out of the way and enable your team to take on certain items in your schedule? Is there sufficient time in your schedule for genuine two-way communication and engagement? Are you scheduled to do things and attend meetings because that is just what happens in your organization? If so, challenge it. You are here to lead – make sure every part of your time is focused on active leadership and not passive acceptance of the status quo.

Don't forget that one of the first aspects of getting out of the way is understanding yourself. Ensure that your schedule allows for and prioritizes you. Do you have enough time for self-reflection and growth?

STEP 3: DEVELOPING AND MATURING YOUR INTENTION WITH YOUR SCHEDULE (OPTIONAL)

Once you have studied your schedule and become intentional about how you are spending your precious and valuable time, you can take your intention one step further. In addition to annotating your upcoming schedule with the seven aspects of leadership, you can be intentional about which vantage points you may want to stay focused on in each different interaction (and indeed how much of your schedule affords you the opportunity to visit and spent time in each vantage point).

From performing this exercise myself, I know that there is a recurring theme I have to watch for, and that is giving myself sufficient space and time in my schedule to spend time in amongst. Partly this is because my schedule fills up with meetings that take me away from the floor walk, or simply observing and watching, and partly it is because I am more of an introvert by nature and therefore I know I have to plan interaction like this otherwise it won't just happen because I won't by preference seek it out.

This exercise is worth repeating every three months or so to help you remain intentional about how you are spending your time. It is the most practical of the tools. It's all very well to read this book, understand it intellectually and have the best of plans to implement its principles in your working life. But your schedule will always pull you back to the way things are and mean you never quite have enough time just yet. Time is there. Creating conscious intention means it is within your gift to make choices about how you prioritize and use that time.

DON'T BE AFRAID OF THE DARK: FEEDBACK

Surely if we can't see something, it's not there, right? Wrong! How people experience us and feel about us as leaders is very much there. We can choose to ignore it and pretend it's not there. But it is. We may as well join the party, shine a light, get uncomfortable and ask.

I started this book by stating that leadership is a choice – not by us but by others. Think about how you have felt about some of the best and worst leaders you have worked with. You chose in your heart how you viewed them completely and entirely based on how you and others experienced their leadership – and others will judge you in the same way, whether you choose to look for and understand that experience or not.

There are many ways to seek feedback. My wish for you as a leader is that you embrace and have as many of these open to you as possible, so that you can truly be experienced the way you hope or intend to be. And starting from the perspective that leadership is about others and not about you immediately has the power to diffuse the risk that you may worry that feedback is personal. If your leadership is truly about others, then this realization helps to move your centre out of your own ego and into being the best servant that you can to others.

Many organizations will have formalized feedback processes, whether they are performance reviews, 360-degree feedback tools, skip-level meetings, surveys or other formats. All of these areas of gathering feedback are helpful and provide different perspectives that can be hugely important. If you have access to more sophisticated psychometric tests and assessment tools, take them. There are a multitude available. They will serve to widen your window of awareness and enable you to respond in such a way that your experience of yourself or your intention matches more closely the experience people have of you.

I have worked with many leaders who fear feedback. They are concerned that who they are and how they wish to be are not reflected in others' views. Therefore, they either believe it is better not to know or believe that the 'others' must be wrong as they don't understand. Whatever the reason, it simply isn't relevant. Leadership is how other people experience us and we must be prepared to face that and be open to adjusting, changing, being vulnerable, and exposing more of our own feelings and failures in order to create mutual understanding. The very act of seeking feedback and sharing it will create respect and greater equality and partnership between leaders and teams. No one is expecting a leader to be perfect.

I have also worked with many leaders who believe they already get all the feedback they need. They tell people that they have an open-door policy and that people can tell them anything, and then they assume that people are telling them the truth (whether they are or not) and just carry on. The problem for everyone in these situations is that genuine feedback is being shared – but it's being shared at the 'water cooler' between team members and not with the leader at all, meaning that everyone ends up powerless to change anything. Even the most genuinely accessible of us can't rely on others to really tell us the truth. They may fear for themselves if they share feedback which is developmental for you. They may fear for your feelings and want to protect you. So having multiple ways of understanding whether your leadership is experienced as you intend is literally the basis for all good leaders. If you are afraid of the dark, don't take on a leadership position. You owe it to the one or tens of thousands of people who work with you to shine that light, get uncomfortable, know it is all about others and be prepared to make changes.

My suggestions are straightforward in terms of feedback and making this part of your practice:

- Make it easier on yourself and help others to learn how to give feedback by framing your questions with a positive approach (e.g. "What did I do well/less well?" or "What would make this work even better?")

- Include a regular feedback schedule that is anonymized (e.g. incorporating surveys, 360-degree feedback and assessment tools) – this way, you will be able to understand themes in aggregate and gather often fantastic verbatim comments that tell you what to do more of and what to do less of

- Cultivate a culture of trust by asking for feedback all the time, thanking people graciously, telling them what you did as a result of their feedback and helping to always make it safe for them to say what they think and feel

- Act comfortably – this is not about manipulating anything, but if people see you as uncomfortable or resistant to feedback, they simply won't give it to you; so be aware and smile, be reflective, be calm and try to keep your emotions in check so they don't leak!

- Seek a reverse mentor, who might be someone in your team with whom you wouldn't ordinarily come in close contact on an everyday basis and who may have a very different perspective – this is a great opportunity to learn and not only gain feedback but also widen and broaden your vantage points

And remember – feedback is just that! It isn't necessarily true. It is a reflection of someone else's experience measured against their expectations. It is information that you can distil and from which you can take what is useful for you, although this isn't an excuse to ignore the things you don't want to hear. If you spend sufficient time with the inside vantage point, then you truly become able to pick out the feedback that might be hard to hear but that you know to be true.

MIRROR, MIRROR

This tool does not involve stepping into Snow White and a fairy tale, although the principle of being prepared to see what the mirror reflects back is probably similar. The 'mirror, mirror' exercise is particularly uncomfortable for some and takes a while to get used to; however, it is a very useful tool if you want to understand more about how you are experienced by others.

Effectively, it involves practising intention versus experience. This is particularly useful if you are preparing to share information and are genuinely interested in doing as much as you can to help your intended messaging reach and be heard by others. It is also helpful when preparing for engagements with other people of any kind. This is by far one of the simplest and most practical tools available to anyone.

Stand in front of a mirror (make it a full-length mirror if you can, because communication and people's experience of us involve our whole body language, not just our face). Look at yourself and speak to the mirror as if you are having a conversation or delivering your presentation. Try different ways of standing. Try smiling. Try pausing. Are you offering an opportunity for others to speak or are you on 'transmit'?

Use the mirror as if you are practising a part in a play. Consider different responses to what you are saying and consider how you might approach, alter or change the way you are speaking or even what you are saying. Can you facilitate a coaching moment, allowing you to listen more? Are your body language and your facial expression serious? Inviting? Compassionate? What are you trying to convey that is in support of others?

The mirror, mirror exercise doesn't have to be done in front of a mirror – you could use a video or live screen, or you could practise with another person. You could even just practise without visual feedback from a reflection or image, although this is less powerful.

The benefit of the mirror, mirror exercise is that you provide yourself with space to think about your impact, to be intentional and then to be open to noticing how you might be experienced by others by effectively putting yourself in other people's shoes. The key is to try not to sit in judgement or make any assumptions about how you believe someone else will be or will respond to you. Think about possible scenarios, but concentrate on how you experience yourself. I promise, it gets easier the more you expose yourself to you. Following are some examples of when speaking and looking into a mirror may be helpful:

- Preparing for a presentation (is it boring or engaging?)
- Preparing for a difficult one-to-one conversation
- Preparing for how you intend to 'show up' as you meet a focus group or team (are you nervous? How might that show up and then how might it be experienced? Can you put a smile on your face?)

- Preparing to listen to something factual and intense that you need to digest – find a recording that is similar to or mimics whatever you will hear, and then watch yourself listening to it. What is your resting expression? Do you have a furrowed brow as you take in information? How might others experience this? Can you become aware of your face and relax it?

If, as a leader, you have ever been exposed to acting classes or presentation training via actors, the mirror, mirror exercise will remind you of that approach. It is about learning to relax with yourself, learning to see yourself as others do, and learning to play for the audience and not for yourself.

SET INTENTIONS: THE 'THREE THINGS' EXERCISE (OR OBITUARY EXERCISE)

I love this one! It's really a very simple and helpful tool, not only to support the creation of clarity but also to give you something tangible to test against your vantage points. The idea here is to firmly place yourself in the future and then work backwards to today, essentially with the purpose of creating an anchor or 'North Star' to help guide you directionally.

First, stop what you are doing. Turn off your computer and find a quiet space with a blank piece of paper. If you have the job description for your role or the original job advertisement, this is a useful thing to have to hand and read.

Imagine that an amount of time has passed – perhaps three years. You could choose a different time frame, but if you do make it longer – up to five years. I always think three years is the shortest time that works for this exercise as leadership usually takes three years to have an impact (in year one, observing, designing and articulating strategy and direction; in year two, the messy implementation; and in year three, tidying up, consolidating and embedding).

At that point in three years' time, what is it that you want to have achieved? What will others say and know you have achieved? Write down three things. As you write these three things, try to keep these three principles in mind:

1. **SHORT.** Write a brief sentence describing what you have done.

2. **SPECIFIC.** Exactly what will you have achieved? For example, a productivity increase of X%? An employee engagement increase of Y%?

3. **SHIFT.** Make sure those statements move something and create significant impact.

Now, put your list of three things somewhere visible – perhaps printed and put up on a wall, or it could be your screensaver. But make sure it is somewhere you will be reminded daily of those three things. Regularly review your calendar, your commitments and the way you spend your time, and decide whether you are genuinely working towards those three things every day, every week and making progress. This consistent focus will ensure you have something to show for your leadership efforts, and will keep you out of the way of the day-to-day aspects of your job that stand in the way of you making significant progress.

Having these three things clearly stated will also help you to create clarity, and you can use them as a reference as you journey forward. And, as you use your five vantage points, you can bounce what you are observing and seeing against the three things to ensure you are staying on track. This doesn't mean to say that the three things will be the only ones you will do and focus on, but they will help you to prioritize and ensure that they *do* happen.

VISION-BOARDING

Much has been written and researched about vision-boarding, or "action boarding," as Dr Tara Swart refers to it in her wonderful book *The Source*. She writes, "An action board will be the ultimate manifestation of priming your brain to design your life. The fact that you create it with your own hands and see it every day in full colour activates numerous pathways in your brain (tactile, visual, emotional, intuitive and motivational), sending them the core message about what you truly want far more powerfully than just reading a list or thinking about your goals from time to time will ever do."[28]

As with the previous exercise, you need a space away from your usual desk or workspace and distractions. And you need a large, blank piece of paper, a stack of magazines and media, scissors and glue. (You can do this exercise virtually on any electronic platform with digital images as well, but I find it much more powerful and creative to do physically.)

You can create a vision or action board for anything: for your whole life, for a specific aspect of your life, whatever you want to aim for. This again is all about creating clarity. Look for images or words that stand out to you and that you are drawn to. Don't think too much about it. Cut them out, stick them onto your paper and start building what is effectively a collage that represents your deepest interests and desires. You can spend a few days coming back to this and building it until you have a picture that excites you, motivates you, makes you smile and feels aspirational. Having this clarity with regard to your own values will be useful for you as you lead others and show up with authenticity.

Place the picture somewhere where you will see it every day – perhaps somewhere by your workspace, where you will see it all the time, or somewhere close to where you sleep, so you see it on waking and going to bed. Some people have been known to put their vision board on their ceiling above their bed! Seeing this picture all the time, particularly last thing at night, means that your brain will be working on those images, reinforcing them and creating connections related to them during your sleeping hours.

The repetition of a visual image that is aspirational to us primes our brain to seek out and respond to opportunities and creates focus and clarity that are largely unconscious. It's deeply effective – I happen to be writing a book because of mine!

BESPOKE DESIGN

This is a tool for those who like to plan and structure things in a visual way. It will hopefully create a sense of clarity for you but also a sense of 'place'. Much of what the previous chapters have said about clarity, getting out of the way and leveraging your vantage points might seem like you need to redesign the way you approach leadership and how you perceive the essence and fabric of your job role. I hope so. I'm keen to encourage you to do the leading and to create the collective agency in others, rather than being caught up in a busy schedule of meetings, reporting, trying to get people to do what you need them to do, but not always being clear yourself and then dealing with stakeholder challenges and demands. Bespoke design is here as a tool in your toolkit to 'redecorate' – or reimagine your space.

Imagine those moments when you walk into a room that you know well. The furniture is in the same place, the decoration is the same and there is a walkway down the side of the room – but perhaps it feels cluttered, so perhaps you don't use that room very much? Then think about those TV programmes where a designer comes in, understands the needs of the client and designs something completely different. There is then a big reveal moment at the end of the show where the client can't believe it's the same room! You can do this too – you might discover a whole new way of using your 'leadership space' in just as drastic a way.

DESIGN JOB 1: YOUR NEEDS FOR THE SPACE. I have hopefully helped you with the contents of the book with this one, and you can add your own texture of course. But make a list of the things you need to be able to do with your leadership space – don't start editing and taking things out at this point. That is like saying, "I really want a comfortable chair for cosy reading space in my living room but the current couch is too big and there isn't enough space." (The current couch won't be there! Just put down that you want reading space.). Note that some things that you need for the space may already be present in your current space. Bespoke design includes all the great things you have already.

DESIGN JOB 2: CLEAR THE ROOM. You could metaphorically do this by taking a blank sheet of paper, a blank calendar or anything else to represent blank space.

DESIGN JOB 3: PRIORITIZE YOUR LIST OF NEEDS OR GIVE THEM SCALE. For example, you might put monthly focus groups with employees first, followed by networking events, reflection time, etc. and the duration of each activity. If you are very visual, using graph paper and cutting out pieces of paper that represent each aspect you wish to introduce at a scaled size can help you to see how things fit in – exactly like in room design. It also leads to creative solutions – no space for two single beds? How about bunk beds? In the instance of leadership, this might mean doubling up on some activities. For example, you could take some team members along to a networking event and use the time to gather external information and feedback as well as have discussions and engage with the team.

DESIGN JOB 4: CHECK FOR BALANCE. As you perfect how to fit all your needs into your space and you prioritize what you can and can't do (remembering to leave some space for spontaneity, rest, unforeseen activity, etc.), look for a balance. You should be looking for a balanced portfolio of intentional activity that is about clarity, getting out of the way and spending time in each of the five vantage points.

DESIGN JOB 5: LIVE IN THE SPACE. Live in the redesigned space for a bit before you bolt the furniture to the floor. The point here is to be flexible – you want to be able to move the chair if the lovely reading corner that you were seeking isn't in quite the right light. Or if you find that your priorities shift once you start living in your new leadership space.

DESIGN JOB 6: REFLECT UPON WHAT IS NO LONGER IN THE SPACE. We have all been in this situation – we finally get rid of the piece of furniture that was left to us by Granny that we didn't really use and that didn't go with our style but we felt we needed to hold on to it because otherwise when Mum came round she would have asked where it was. Do you miss it? If so, find a way of putting it back in. If not, it's your space, not anyone else's, so take a picture for the memories and then sell or gift the furniture to someone else or repurpose it in another room. But don't let other people's ideas of what is important for your leadership space dominate, meaning that the things that are important to you don't have room. For example, there might be a weekly meeting that your predecessor went to that shows up on your calendar and takes two hours out of your diary. You don't know why you go or whether it serves your main job, which is to create clarity and get out of the way in order to foster collective agency in your team, to facilitate their ability to deliver progress in moving from A to B. If that meeting does not contribute to that purpose, don't go. Delegate it. Change it. But do not allow that piece of furniture into your leadership space because one piece will lead to another and before you know it, you'll have lost your bespoke design and will be living in someone else's space.

DESIGN JOB 7: SHOW OFF YOUR SPACE AND SHARE IT. I have talked a lot throughout this book about sharing the view (see especially *Chapter 2*) and I have also talked about inviting others into your unique vantage points. Leadership is a team sport and a shared activity. Leadership doesn't exist without others, so be transparent and bring them in to your space. If they understand the importance of this bookshelf or that cosy corner, they will respect the work that you are prioritizing as a leader and they can be part of supporting you, as you will support them.

Enjoy creating your bespoke leadership space. This space is where we can find inspiration, thrive and flourish. Your leadership space should be intentional and curated with care and should help you to fulfil the 'being' of your leadership (see *Chapter 5*). As with all design, be creative and be you.

CREATE STORIES: JOURNAL AT THE END OF EVERY DAY

I was once given a really good piece of advice about reflection and self-awareness. Many people journal and write to help get their feelings on paper or to make a record of what is happening in their lives. The advice I was given was to use this tool to help to create, develop and demonstrate stories. The purpose of recording these stories is to help your leadership practice through longer-term reflection and looking for patterns and progress.

The aim is not to write an essay. The aim is just to write a brief paragraph every day without thinking too much about it, noting things that happened, feelings, etc. Then just put it away.

The power of journaling in this way is the reflection that it allows at a distance. It is a bit like baking bread, making wine or any such process that involves waiting for the goods.

Journal in this way for three to six months. Try not to keep going back and reading what you have previously written – just keep it up and write something every day. Then, after six months, keep writing, but go back and read your first three months of journal entries. Enough time will have passed that these will feel fairly removed from you, and you will be able to read them with some objectivity.

Remember that the outcome you are looking for is to practise accessing and leveraging all five vantage points and, by doing so, to fulfil the two key jobs of a leader, which are to create clarity and to get out of the way. When you read your old entries, you are looking for evidence of your perspective. What evidence can you find in what you wrote that you were accessing the five vantage points? Does it seem like you were favouring one or two more than others? What evidence is there that you were creating clarity or getting out of the way? On reflection, could you have done more or approached things differently? How were you spending your time? This is in a way an extended version of the diary check tool earlier in this chapter.

You can be scientific about this and literally tally up evidence as you find it to see what this tells you about what you have recorded. Alternatively, you might just like to keep the desired outcomes in your mind as you read through, reflecting on your observations. It doesn't matter how you choose to conduct your reflection, but it will likely tell you something you can learn from and build into your practice moving forward. It will start to tell you the stories that make up your experiences, and you can use these stories to reflect on what happened. Note that if you try to recall what happened without daily recording, it is likely that you will selectively remember things or retrospectively amend them based on your present opinions.

The other way, or additional way, that you can use this journaling stories approach is to read through your entries from the different vantage points. So, instead of looking at the record for evidence of whether you accessed the five perspectives equally or at all, read through it *from* those perspectives and think about what that might tell you and what it draws out for you in terms of insight.

Repeat the exercise in another three months with the next section of your journal entries.

This tool effectively gives you a special sixth vantage point that is only accessible to you through active reflection, and that is your future self. This means looking back and observing from a different time point so as to more objectively view the occurrences and feelings that you recorded.

Hindsight. It's a wonderful thing. But only useful if we apply it to our practice intentionally in the future.

THE VANTAGE POINT COMMUTE: MORNING ROUTINE

Many people are increasingly talking about the benefit of a morning routine – time set aside each morning to take care of yourself and become centred for the day ahead. For some, this is a morning run, yoga session, meditation or simply the routine of making a cup of coffee and savouring drinking it for a quiet moment.

This is a really good moment to take the opportunity to journey to your different vantage points as a leader and consider the day ahead – a morning 'commute,' if you like, around the different perspectives that each of the five vantage points may afford. My recommendation would be that journeying around the vantage points should not be a substitute for any self-care or self-centring morning routine that you have, but it might be a nice addition before you dive into the day.

You may be familiar with the mindfulness technique of a 'body scan,' where you find a quiet spot where you won't be disturbed and take your attention in turn through each part of your body, noticing it, noticing any aches and pains or where a certain part of your body touches your chair, and moving on throughout your whole body. It's a way of keeping in touch with your physical self and bringing mindful attention to it. This both calms the mind and helps with connection between mind and body.

The vantage point commute is a similar concept in a way. It really is about setting intention and providing you with an opportunity to remember all these different perspectives and be intentional about how you are going to conduct your day ahead with these in mind. I would suggest that there are two quick journeys that are beneficial:

1. **THE BIGGER-PICTURE COMMUTE.** Think about your mission, where you are headed and what you are trying to achieve holistically in your organization, with your purpose – your 'where are we going?' from *Chapter 2* (or your 'three things' exercise from this section). Journey around the five vantage points whilst keeping that bigger picture and ambition in your mind. What do you notice at each stopping-off point? If you head to in amongst, what is coming up? If you bring yourself back out and up to from high out and beyond, what do you see today? Just observe.

2. **THE DAY AHEAD.** Think about your day ahead and what you have planned for the coming six to ten hours. Again, in the context of the different vantage points, think about the meetings, connections and work outputs that will be required. From which perspective do you want to intentionally approach each meeting, collaboration or decision that is happening today? Decide where you are going to sit and from which vantage point you want to approach each particular aspect of your day. Take a moment to think about these activities in advance from your different perspectives so you are already prepared with those observations and thought-starters to keep you intentional and thoughtful about the day ahead.

If you build this practice into your day (it can literally only take minutes, or longer if you so wish), you will already have anchored your brain in the practice of sitting in the respective vantage points you have intentionally considered in the morning. And you are more likely to automatically go there and leverage those perspectives during your busy day. As a consequence, it won't feel like an additional thing that you have to keep considering and thinking about. Rather, you set your intention and it plays out in your experience throughout the day.

BONUS ACTIVITY 1. With this vantage point commute, there is a quick and useful bonus activity. Grab a piece of paper and a pen, and as soon as you have completed the two parts of your journey, write down very briefly what you will do today to create more clarity and what you will do today to get out of the way (based on what you learned as you took part in your commute). This is another way of setting and anchoring intention into your day.

BONUS ACTIVITY 2. Why not try the vantage point 'commute home' at the end of the day? Flip the practice and spend a few minutes reflecting on your day and journeying around your vantage points, considering what you observe about what happened and how you spent your day. And then take the bigger picture and do the same, reflecting on what you are trying to achieve from different perspectives. Again, jotting down how you created clarity today and how you got out of the way closes the loop on this reflection.

THE ANGEL ON YOUR SHOULDER: EMOTIONAL AWARENESS

I've been thinking about this angel for some time. Bear with me – this tool won't be for everyone, but I rather like it and felt I should include it as an option. Being aware of how we are feeling and what emotions we are experiencing is hugely valuable as a leader. Everyone, sometimes especially leaders, should feel whatever they feel. It's what we do with that emotion and whether we can notice it sufficiently to choose how we harness the emotions that is really important. Emotional responses left unchecked in a leader can mean others experience them in less optimal ways. They can really affect whether others experience the clarity or the getting out of the way that the leader is trying to achieve. This tool is designed to help us notice and see our emotions, which in itself enables us to create sufficient pause time to make choices about how and whether we want to harness those emotions.

Picture a small angel, fluttering by your right shoulder (mine is female so I'll describe her as such, but yours can be gendered or genderless – however the idea manifests for you). Really look at her. What is she wearing? How big are her wings? She needs to be close, so imagine her right there, sitting between your shoulder and your ear. Imagine she is always there. Try to think about your angel each day. Look for her, imagine her and start to observe her more closely.

Your angel is there to help you understand how you are feeling. She might be fluttering around, very relaxed and calm. She might be beating her wings quickly, flying erratically. Or she might be darting about, excitable and full of energy. Keep checking in with your angel and try to get used to noticing her and taking a moment to check in with her.

Visualizing your angel has the potential to help you in three main ways:

1. In order to check in with your angel, you need to stop for a moment. You need to come out of yourself and focus your attention on observing something exterior to you. This very act of stopping and looking for your angel halts your reactive processes and provides you with valuable breathing space to pause and make choices.

2. Your angel is good. She is kind and she is on your side. No emotion is to be judged and she is beyond judgement. She is there to be observed, and observed with compassion. As an extension to this, you can share that compassion with yourself. It's OK to be worried and it's ok to be angry or upset. Nothing is invalid when it comes to feelings – they just are.

3. The very act of noticing and observing your angel has the power to change things for you and for her. By observing your angel with curiosity and compassion, you may find that she gradually reduces that frantic wing-beating, and you may find that she softens in her furious responses or brightens up from gloom. We all need to feel acknowledged and noticed, and the very act of noticing her may help those feelings to regulate themselves even just a little – maybe just long enough to create space for a choice in your own behaviour.

Of course, the angel on your shoulder is a metaphor for your own self-awareness. It is about building the skill and the practice of checking in with your own feelings so you are in control rather than your emotions ruling your behaviour, which can feel challenging and unsatisfactory for you and for those you work with and alongside.

The angel on your shoulder is particularly powerful as part of your inside vantage point, but she is also very helpful to have alongside you as you move between the five vantage points. You may find that she helps you to notice feelings that are different as you spend time in each of these different perspectives. Perhaps you feel fully at home, calm and happy when you are in amongst because that is where you have spent most of your career and you love the camaraderie and the familiar work and setting? When you spend time observing from high above, do you feel lonely? Do you feel out of your depth? When you are observing from high out and beyond, do you feel like an imposter and anxious? Notice how the angel on your shoulder is feeling in these different settings. Noticing what is happening with her can help you to acknowledge these feelings, look at them, bring them into the light and make choices and decisions, seek support and notice your preferences. For example, if you feel really calm and happy when you are in amongst, you may find you favour this vantage point over others and that you spend a disproportionate amount of your time in this space because other vantage points feel less comfortable.

PERSPEX TOOLBOX

Be visible about your tools and the way you lead. These are not to be kept hidden away somewhere whilst outwardly you push forward with alpha behaviour – share your approach visibly and with vulnerability.

Often, leaders find that they are not getting out of the way enough because it is not clear to others how they are leading, what they are prioritizing or what works for them. Greater transparency is always a good thing when trying to build trust and understanding, and the Perspex toolbox is a great way of thinking about this.

What might this mean in practice? It might mean that you start to state more openly that you are going to use data and reporting as a way of keeping on top of the status of a certain project. Once the person who is writing long narrative reports knows this, you can have an open discussion about what works for you and whether they have the skills required to change their reporting style. You can then agree how to ensure that you both get what you need. This might mean that you share openly with people that you are not a fan of the phone. You might prefer to work with email and text communication because it means you aren't interrupted and that you have focused time and can get to all those messages as and when you are available.

If everyone you work with can see the tools of your trade, how you work and how you like to lead, then they can ensure they are ready to respond and ready to work with you. The chances are that this may motivate others to start to use Perspex toolboxes as well, which will increase your insight! With that transparency, you can understand why person X does the things they do in the way they do. It might be frustrating to you, or it might seem illogical because you don't do it that way, but being able to see helps to create open discussion and visual clues, and these in turn generate understanding. It also helps people to help you. If people know that you have certain ways of working, they can anticipate your needs and can also provide you with suggestions and feedback. They may even notice the tools that you don't have or aren't using, and help you to bring those into your toolbox.

TEACHER'S TRICK

This is a coaching method designed to keep you as a leader out of 'directive' mode, where you feel you need to have the answers. Instead, you can create the space for others to work things out for themselves and build their problem-solving muscles. Just asking the simple question of "What do you think?" and then actively listening is a key means for you to get out of the way.

One way of teaching is for teachers to impart information to students and the students to absorb that information in a passive way. However, we know that whilst this may mean that the students learn the specific information at hand, they are not challenged to create the skills and master the techniques required for research, self-directed learning, problem-solving and lateral thinking. And the students are reliant on the teacher to provide the information, which they passively receive. As a leader, do you want your team to wait for your direction, to be dependent on the next instruction, and to look to you for all the thought leadership and problem-solving? That would be exhausting for any leader! It would keep you well away from being able to access any vantage point except in amongst because you would constantly be required by your team. Instead, hit the tennis ball back over the net by asking questions, and make them play another shot. It will build fitness, agility, skills and creativity. Help people to get used to coming to you for the 'bounce' and not the answer.

Asking "What do you think?" is also very helpful when you literally don't know the answer (which I believe teachers don't sometimes) and is a much better response than making something up because you feel as a leader that you should know everything! By the time you have heard what others think in a room of 15 people when you didn't initially know what to say yourself, you will have 15 better solutions and ideas to add to your consideration and to broaden your thinking. Also, this simple question works really well if you want to bring someone up to your vantage point. Taking an individual or team from in amongst to any of the other external vantage points and asking "What do you think?" will enable you to expand what you can see. Take people who are like you and people who are not like you. Ask more people, more often: "What do you think?"

THE COACH INSIDE YOU

This is one of my favourite tools. The role of a mentor or coach is to provide wisdom, guidance and advice. Many people in leadership positions benefit from having mentors or coaches throughout their careers, and the encouragement, challenge and support that they often provide can create pivotal moments of enlightenment and self-awareness. We often consult a mentor or coach when we are in need of support to work through a difficult decision or when we need to process or handle a situation.

What you might not realize is that you can access your own inner wisdom right inside yourself. It is a variation on your inside vantage point. If you think about it when you take coaching, the role of the coach is to bring out your own inner understanding and help you explore options, but these are generated largely from your own experience, perspectives and insights.

Think of yourself in the future, and imagine that your future self is meeting you, today. Imagine your future self asking questions which help you to think about your current situation, maybe a problem you are aiming to overcome. The point of the future self is to position yourself with some distance from your current situation and to challenge, provide advice, or it might be to share guidance. What would you say to yourself? Take a pen and paper and write down words, draw pictures, make a record or journal anything that you feel you need to in the immediate moments after you have 'met with yourself' and capture the inner wisdom inside yourself.

We all have the ability to access our innermost wisdom in this way – pausing, creating space and asking ourselves for the important clues that may help to guide our intuition and support our decision-making. This is a meditative, powerful way of accessing your inside vantage point. And you don't have to make an appointment – the coach is inside whenever you need them.

A similar approach is outlined in *Playing Big* by Tara Mohr.[29] (It's in chapter two in Mohr's book. If you want the full description, including a guided visualization, I encourage you to read her book or visit her website, where you can experience the Virtual Mentor guided visualization.)

Chapter 8

TROUBLESHOOTING

So, you have read through and understood the critical opportunity that vantage points offer to you as a leader, and you hopefully now buy in to the concept of the leader's role being to create clarity and get out of the way. You have perhaps even committed to building and growing your leadership practice in support of this leadership philosophy, which puts others first. But it's not all plain sailing. Here are five examples of challenges that you might face and some quick troubleshooting advice to help you through.

I'M A LEADER BUT I'M ALSO A DO-ER – I'M IN MIDDLE MANAGEMENT!

This is often a challenging place to be as a leader as you are trying to stretch your leadership wings and to develop a focus on supporting and enabling your team and leading through others, and yet you also have delivery objectives and outcomes that you have to focus on and that are expected of you. You might, alternatively, be a team leader of a specialist group where you do not exclusively lead the team as your entire role and you deliver as well. Many people in professional service functions find themselves in this position.

In this instance, there are four points I think are worth taking into account:

1. How you structure and design your time and role is critical. Using some of the suggested tools in *Chapter 7* (such as 'Diary check' or 'Bespoke design'), you can keep a focus on your deliverables whilst also ensuring that there is sufficient space for you to lead in the way you like to lead. Double up some of your delivery time with some in amongst observations.

2. Accept and embrace the dual nature of your work. Rather than seeing the fact that you have these two priorities and spaces as a tension where you may feel that you are not servicing either to the best of your ability, let go of that view of perfection and just do the best. Make sure to constantly give yourself space for reflection and review to ensure that you are prioritizing the key aspects of your leadership role.

3. Vantage points are your friends in this situation. Consciously thinking about balancing your time across the different perspectives is another way of keeping and maintaining harmony when switching between leadership and your own individual contribution.

4. Communicate with your team, and find a way of signalling when you are in your individual contributor space and when you are in your leadership space. This will be helpful for everyone – it might be about where you physically sit or about blocking off time in your calendar with a code. There are many ways others can support you and respect those boundaries.

I GET THIS, BUT I AM WORKING FOR SOMEONE WHO DOES NOT PRACTISE LEADERSHIP LIKE THIS!

Well, let's face it, this is very likely to happen. There are some wonderful leaders out there, some of whom have taught me many of the great tips and practices in this book over the years, but I very commonly hear this feedback when leaders engage in learning and growth and then return to the workplace only to be frustrated that they do not experience this leadership for themselves. They may feel their organization's overall culture is set up to support this way of working.

This is not an easy situation to be in, so we need to start with a fundamental question. I always ask this question as a coach when someone finds themselves in this kind of situation, because essentially handling and managing the situation is all about acknowledging it and taking an active choice. The fundamental question is: can I live with the leader that I have or can I not? If I can't exist and thrive and find ways of working well or even with acceptance of the situation, then my choice must surely be that I need to move and take my talents elsewhere to work in a situation where I can thrive. If I can't move right away, but I commit to moving in a two-year time horizon, for example, then I need to think through how I can create the best possible situation for myself in that time period and serve the people who work with and around me to the best of my ability. If I do not choose to leave at any point, then at a minimum I need to accept the situation.

Acceptance is the removal of the word 'should.' A very wise leader I worked with and learned much from once encouraged me, as a very frustrated leader in my early years of senior stakeholder management, to lose the word 'should' from my vocabulary. He helped me to see that acceptance is realizing that whilst things should or shouldn't be a certain way or people should or shouldn't be a certain way, they are. People and things are as they are. And once we accept that, we provide ourselves with a much less frustrating landscape, the storm clouds start to disappear, and we can see clearly how we can work within the situation as it is and with the people as they are, not how we may imagine they 'should' be. If we are not prepared to move on from the situation, then we need to think about how we can choose to accept it. This then opens up lots of possibility for us to collaborate and lead with compassion for everyone, including our leaders. Therefore, I would suggest two ways of moving on from acceptance and building your practice as you like to lead:

1. Be compassionate to your leader rather than sitting in judgement of them at all times (this is hard!). Try. Compassion enables you to move forward with them, whilst judgement is sticky and enables none of this momentum.

The main question to ask is: "What does my leader need most from me and how can I service this, such that I have the autonomy and freedom to lead as I choose?" (You can observe your leader and work this out yourself or ask directly.) You need to service the needs of your leader. Another way of building compassion for your leader and enabling your space to be effective is to invite them in. I have noticed that, sometimes, when people have micromanaging bosses (for example) or leaders who display some behaviours that do not sit comfortably with them, they create avoidance. I find this can make things worse. Bring your leader in close, invite them to join in to see your performance and success, give them a job to do (e.g. ask them to speak at an event, or invite them to review the work of a team or be part of a celebration) and provide positive reinforcement of their contribution.

2. Be confident and results oriented in your approach. Deliver. If you and your team are delivering because you have performed your role as leader by effectively setting the scene with clarity and engaging with stakeholders through a stakeholder map and actively communicating two-way, then how you deliver will be more open to you as a choice.

I FEEL ALONE – THIS IS SURELY THE JOB OF A SUPERHERO

Leadership can be lonely at times. However, there are various ways of building support so that in actual fact you are the curator of a leadership posse. In her many books researcher and author Brené Brown talks of embracing vulnerability and not feeling like we have to do everything at all times. In *The Gifts of Imperfection* she says of the difference between healthy striving and perfectionism: "Healthy striving is self-focussed – *How can I improve?* Perfectionism is other-focussed – *What will they think?*"[30] Firstly, build your support network around you. As a leader, you need your HR or people business partner, a finance business partner, and IT support and help. These three functional specialisms should be part of your inner circle, often to be found in particular with you at the vantage points of to the side and around and from high above. They should help you to reflect upon the team. Positively and proactively bring them into how you build clarity, and use professionals to help guide you and coach you with their advice. Legal advice is also at times required and, depending on your role, procurement advice as well. Build out a support network of professionals. These people should be your 'critical friends' in support of you but also challenging you based on risk, impact, best practice and so on.

Secondly, build a network of coaches and mentors. I have seen some leaders over the years waiting for a corporate programme to provide them with a mentor or a coach. These programmes may be fine, but my advice is to build this yourself over time. Find people you admire and ask their advice, and create relationships where you can reflect with someone else who can take the burden of asking the questions so you can relax into reflection fully. Make sure to look for people who are different to you and, where possible, find a reverse mentor within your organization who can help you to experience being in amongst in a different way whilst also providing you with some guidance and advice as a leader.

Invest in a coach. You may feel that your organization should always pay for every piece of development that you undertake, but you may end up missing out on your own growth if you wait. Own your growth as an investment in yourself and your leadership impact and career. I have often funded my own coaching in order to unlock some of my thinking and support me as part of my network and resilience.

Thirdly, read, stay curious and read some more. There are so many ways to keep up to speed and digest content now as a leader, whether it is through podcasts, blogs, journals, books or other publications. These resources are fantastic at helping you to shape your thinking, bounce around your reflections, feel less alone and stretched, and feel more supported, and leaders need to be digesting great content as part of a continual curious practice.

Finally, let go of perfection. I have talked about feeling compassion for your leader if they don't make the grade all the time, but be compassionate to yourself too! What I outline in this book is the best practice I have observed, and I use it to guide leaders I work with. But none of us can be expected to be all of this all of the time. We are human, too. Be good enough. Focus on clarity and getting out of the way as a mantra to guide you as you muddle through, and bring your team in when you are feeling more vulnerable or less sure. The humble leader will be lifted up by the team – they want you to be amazing! And they will think you are even more so when you appear just a little more 'like them' by asking for help.

THIS ALL SOUNDS GREAT, BUT I DON'T HAVE TIME!

Go back and read the book again. If you have the same question, refer to the following point.

IS LEADERSHIP FOR ME?

This is a wonderful question. And a really important question. It is a question that is not asked often enough by leaders in organizations that are involved with building talent, it is not asked often enough by HR and people professionals, and it is not asked enough by individuals who take on leadership roles throughout their career.

Most people fall into leadership. They don't choose it. Our organizations and institutions are designed such that, if an individual wants to progress with their career and gain more responsibility, autonomy, respect, status, money, etc., very often the only route is 'up.' In the organizations that I work with and for, I advocate in favour of space for people to choose *not* to lead. And for this to be fine. And for those individuals to still be able to grow their influence and their reward and their autonomy and their status. I call this 'mastery.' It might be suitable for someone with a deep interest and technical skill that grows over time. Or someone who simply is not interested in the nuances and human aspects of people leadership – we aren't all interested in this! I have seen countless people in leadership positions over the years – I call them 'accidental leaders' – who have ended up with the responsibility of leading sometimes huge teams of people with little or no natural interest or curiosity in human psychology or human behaviour. Increasingly in the age of technology, AI and robotization of the physical and knowledge work of the 20th century, these people will struggle with the growing requirement to lead humans as opposed to task. Task will be automated, is already automated. It is humans that we need to lead.

This is super-exciting. This is a brilliant point in history as we have come full circle. Industrialization enabled so many positive changes in our societies, but it required us to work for over 100 years to develop the technology to free humans from the physical and task-based knowledge work, such that we are now fully enabled to rely upon the skills and capabilities that have enabled us to be such a successful species over thousands of years. This innate human quality is rooted in creativity, innovation and socialization. When you head back to refresh yourself on the section looking at human beings in *Chapter 5* and the importance of positive psychology and neuroscience, as a leader you really need to be interested and engaged in learning as much as you can about this, because no longer will the task-based approaches to management and leadership be sufficient in the post-industrial age. We are now in the human age.

Leaders need to feel, enable, create clarity, get out of the way and, above all, serve others with an inclusive mindset. Remember, leadership is a choice – not by the leader but by others. What is also true is that leaders themselves need to want to choose human leadership as a passion and vocation, because it is a privilege. When creating clarity, if you are able to focus on others and not yourself, you will be empathetic and therefore a compassionate leader.

If you are looking to gain more reward, more status and more autonomy without developing and constantly practising and growing your understanding of what others need from you, then my suggestion is that you might find yourself better suited to deepening your mastery within your chosen profession or field as an individual contributor. If you can't find time to reimagine your day and week to do the work described in this book and to cultivate the being-ness of a leader, then choose to deepen your mastery as an individual contributor, by doing. People deserve leaders who choose to lead.

CONCLUSION

Leadership can be a complicated job. It's personal because it is all about people. It's messy at times, and it is certainly not a logical or rational occupation all of the time. Data is important but intuition is just as important – they should have equal influence on your approach. A leader who is unable to feel, or who has little emotional intelligence themselves, will find it difficult to connect with and support the enablement of others. So, we start with ourselves, but with the clear understanding that although we start with ourselves, and we use ourselves to create enablement of others, it is never about us.

Our people systems need us to step up. If you are in a leadership position, you need to be ready to be vulnerable, do work on yourself, get uncomfortable and develop the muscle of empathy. Work getting done and people thriving with their needs as humans being met should not be mutually exclusive – and it's no one else's job but that of the leader to bring these two things together.

Seeing leadership as a practice is absolutely critical. None of us is ever the finished article, and it is very easy to slip back into preferences that are unconscious to us, whether that be a technical skill or capability, the discipline we may have as our core pre-leadership profession, or a busy diary keeping us away from reflection and our more strategic leadership purpose. We constantly have to provide ourselves with time, feedback, challenge and attention to our own self-care, in order to ensure that we are performing our two key tasks: creating clarity and getting out of the way.

We have explored the vantage points that a leader has available to them throughout this book by defining each of these and then applying them to the two key jobs of a leader. One final thought about leading in this way is outlined in *Figure 26*, which shows the difference between what I call 'push leadership' and 'magnetic leadership.' If we return to the premise that leaders are chosen, then effective leaders create the energy and inspiration within their teams to act, move, collaborate and get things done.

FIGURE 26: PUSH VERSUS MAGNETIC LEADERSHIP

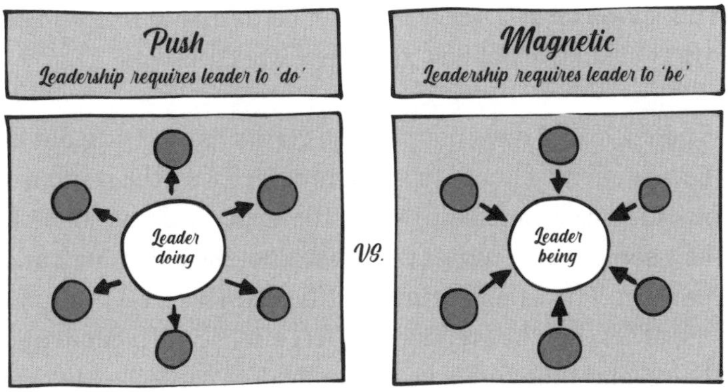

Where people have choice, they are much more likely to be self-starting in their behaviours and actions. Where a leader facilitates clarity and gets out of the way, the aim is to create a kind of magnetic field that attracts the team both individually and collectively. By virtue of this magnetic field, the team then follows the required direction and seeks support, with the leader acting as a central coordinating point for the work of the team. The way the leader is – their 'being' – this creates this attraction.

Where clarity is lacking, the leader is required to push much more, create more detailed direction and provide more corrections because people don't understand the parameters to focus their work around. The leader must continually bring them back to the central purpose as there is more risk of individualized creativity and lack of common activity.

Similarly, where a leader is unable to get out of the way and create the space for individuals and teams to work with a sense of freedom, choice and creativity, a tether is almost required to keep people connected to the work. In *Figure 26* you can imagine this as the leader holding each employee like a hot-air balloon to stop them floating away and to keep the leader in control. This shows up as a heavy focus on performance reviews and strict guidance about how and where work gets done.

Where a leader does not practise clarity and getting out of the way effectively and in a synchronized way, the result is a 'push' form of leadership, where the leader is 'doing' and it is their doing that activates the progress of the individuals and the team. This is suboptimal for the team because there is a lack of space to be creative and feel a sense of freedom and choice (and therefore a lack of individual control, resulting in increased stress and worse performance). And it is sub-optimal for the leader, because it is really time intensive and hard work to control that amount of work, especially when at scale! In fact, it is often impossible. It is also a really diffi-cult pattern to break, because whilst a leader is 'doing' and practising push leadership, there is very little time for them to access all five vantage points, to reflect, and therefore to provide clarity and to get out of the way – there is simply too much to do to get out of the way!

I recall one leader I worked with a few years ago musing on this point and having his own breakthrough moment: "The team and the size of this work for which I am responsible are too big. I simply have no more hours in the day to throw at this. I need to fundamentally change what I do to influence the activities of my group."

As a leader, get up tomorrow and spend more time 'being' and less time 'doing.' It's as good a place to start as any, and you may find those tight tethers that you hold on to with your push style of leadership start to slacken as people are drawn into your energy field. Through your clear direction and your support of them, they may begin to lean into their own agency. The impact and outcomes are powerfully productive and rewarding for all!

Finally, this book is called *Vantage Points* because my aim has been to encourage you to make the most of the perspectives that leadership brings. By understanding these five different ways of seeing your team and the work, and by understand-ing where you may more readily or easily spend your time and where you may need to nurture a stronger presence, you can unlock the potential to enable you and your teams to prosper and thrive.

ENDNOTES

1. Carol Dweck, *Mindset* (New York, Random House, 2006).

2. "Vantage Point" (Collins), accessed 30 September 2020, https://www.collinsdictionary.com/dictionary/english/vantage-point.

3. Simon Sinek, *Start with Why* (London, Penguin Books Ltd, 2018).

4. Matthew Syed, *Rebel Ideas* (London, John Murray, 2020).

5. "Resourcing" (Cambridge Dictionary), accessed 30 September 2020, https://dictionary.cambridge.org/dictionary/english/resourcing.

6. "Evolve" (Cambridge Dictionary), accessed 30 September 2020, https://dictionary.cambridge.org/dictionary/english/evolve.

7. "Leave" (Cambridge Dictionary), accessed 30 September 2020, https://dictionary.cambridge.org/dictionary/english/leave.

8. "Retain" (Cambridge Dictionary), accessed 30 September 2020, https://dictionary.cambridge.org/dictionary/english/retain?q=retaining.

9. "Expectation" (Cambridge Dictionary), accessed 30 September 2020, https://dictionary.cambridge.org/dictionary/english/expectation.

10. Vocabulary.com, accessed September 25, 2020, https://www.vocabulary.com/dictionary/compassion.

11. Penny Tamkin, Gemma Pearson, Wendy Hirsh and Susannah Constable, *Exceeding Expectation: The Principles of Outstanding Leadership* (The Work Foundation, 2010), accessed 30 September 2020, http://towardsoutstandingleadership.com/images/TWF_leadership_research_-_Executive_summary.pdf.

12. Tamkin et al., *Exceeding Expectation*, p. 8.

13. Rangan Chaterjee, *The Stress Solution* (London, Penguin Life, 2018), p. 10.

14. Jeff Hyman, "Why Humble Leaders Make the Best Leaders" (Forbes), last modified 31 October 2018, https://www.forbes.com/sites/jeffhyman/2018/10/31/humility/#583d8be11c80.

15. Jim Collins, *Good to Great* (London, Vintage Publishing, 2004).

16. Douglas McGregor, *The Human Side of Enterprise* (New York, McGraw-Hill, 1960).

17. John J Morse and Jay W Lorsch, "Beyond Theory Y", Harvard Business Review 1970, accessed September 25, 2020, https://hbr.org/1970/05/beyond-theory.

18. Thinkersinresidence, "Professor Martin Seligman Discusses His Foirmula [sic] for Wellbeing: PERMA" (YouTube), last modified 13 December 2012, https://www.youtube.com/watch?v=iK6K_N2qe9Y.

19. Richard H. Thaler and Cass R. Sunstein, *Nudge: Improving Decisions about Health, Wealth and Happiness* (London, Penguin, 2009).

20. Tamkin et al., *Exceeding Expectation*, p. 8.

21. Myers-Briggs Foundation, accessed September 25, 2020, https://www.myersbriggs.org/my-mbti-personality-type/mbti-basics/.

22. "The Sunday Times Best Companies to Work for 2020" (*The Times*, 2020), accessed 30 September 2020, https://appointments.thetimes.co.uk/article/best100companies.

23. Patrick Lencioni, *The Five Dysfunctions of a Team* (San Francisco, John Wiley and Sons, 2002).

24. Amy Edmondson, "Psychological Safety and Learning Behavior in Work Teams," *Administrative Science Quarterly* 44 (1999): 350–383 at p.6.

25. Margaret Heffernan, "Forget the Pecking Order at Work" (TED, 2015), accessed 30 September 2020, https://www.ted.com/talks/margaret_heffernan_forget_the_pecking_order_at_work/transcript?language=en.

26. Peter Senge, *The Fifth Discipline* (New York, Doubleday, 1994).

27. Daniel Goleman, *Emotional Intelligence* (London, Bloomsbury, 1996).

28. Tara Swart, *The Source: Open Your Mind, Change Your Life* (London, Vermillion, 2020) p. 208.

29. Tara Mohr, *Playing Big* (London, Cornerstone, 2015).

30. Brene Brown, *The Gifts of Imperfection* (Minnesota, Hazelden Publishing, 2010) p.56.

ABOUT THE AUTHOR

PAULA LEACH has developed a lifelong passion and interest in the way people work, individually and collaboratively in organizations, to the best of their potential. In particular, Paula believes in the value of positive, human-centered, intentional leadership as the key enabler for individuals and teams to thrive. Over 25 years, Paula has built her experience across global multinational, large public sector and entrepreneurial growth organisations, holding the positions of Chief People Officer at the Home Office and Global Chief People Officer at FDM Group, a growing FTSE 250 Tech Talent Pipeline organisation. She holds an MBA from Henley Business School and is a Fellow of the CIPD. Paula shares her very practical observations and insights having worked with leaders at all levels in a wide range of organisational settings, in her first book *Vantage Points*. Paula now runs her business, Vantage Points Consulting, specializing in her passion for unlocking the potential in people and organisations through coaching and business consulting. She is launching the Vantage Points Foundation in Autumn 2021 to support and mentor young women to launch their dream careers. Paula lives in Kent, UK with her husband, two daughters and two dogs.